My Eclectic Garden

By
Toni Ghazal

Copyright © 2023 by – Toni Ghazal – All Rights Reserved.

It is not legal to reproduce, duplicate, or transmit any part of this document in either electronic means or printed format. Recording of this publication is strictly prohibited.

Table of Contents

Dedication i
Acknowledgement ii
About the Author iii
Introduction 1
Chapter 1: The Mother of All Life 5
Chapter 2: Locating, Planning, Rotating, Intercropping and Garden Styles 15
Chapter 3: Floral Arrangements 27
Chapter 4: Cabbage Big and Small 37
Chapter 5: Chameleon Cabbages 48
Chapter 6: Chilis Or Peppers? 56
Chapter 7: Everyone's Favorite 67
Chapter 8: Scary Potatoes 81
Chapter 9: Roots and More Roots 93
Chapter 10: Summertime Treats 109
Chapter 11: Beans Spell Summer 128
Chapter 12: Green Pearls of the Garden 137
Chapter 13: Salad Bowl of Different Colors 146
Chapter 14: The Vegetable's Answer to the Sponge 166
Chapter 15: Herbs 172
Chapter 16: Recipes 185
Conclusion 205
Bibliography 207
    Websites 212
    Seed Sources 212

Dedication

Anna Prelesnick Bileck and Frances (Sugie) Inez Paxton Fields, my grandmothers. Their addiction to growing plants seeped into me. What a wonderful gift.

Acknowledgement

Special thanks go to my good friends Cynthia Snow and Jeanne Daboval for their time and input in reading the manuscript. I also want to thank my husband, Ralph, for taking the time to produce the images, which, with his help, I have included in this essay.

About the Author

Toni has been a Master Gardener since 2007. She gives both classroom and on-site seminars in her garden. Her love of vegetable gardening had its roots when helping her paternal grandmother in her garden. After graduating from the University of Oklahoma, she has had a garden for 40-plus years in various parts of the world. She now lives in the Pacific Northwest with her husband and their two dogs.

Introduction

Why is my garden different? Let's start with what it is not. It is not a monoculture. I don't keep vegetables grouped, as in all peppers, tomatoes, etc. I don't have nor want neat, long rows of vegetables. That is boring, and it invites trouble. What I do have is an interesting, organized chaos of planting. The placing of plants invites you to wander and discover what is there. It has eye appeal, color variations and displays different gardening styles naturally without the appearance of a concerted effort.

This book is a process of connecting the dots of vegetable gardening. We are all taught the same methods and requirements for gardening no matter what region or USDA zone we call home. It is up to us to tweak all this information and make it fit our niche.

The chapters that follow are a compilation of curiosity, questions, and surprises of my vegetable gardening endeavors. The wins but also the 'near' wins. These 'near' wins are just as important, if not more so, than the wins because it is these results that you question and tweak in the next planting season. My goal is to spark inquisitiveness, interest, and maybe even excitement about vegetables. Hopefully, the next time you look at vegetables sitting on your plate, there will be an acknowledgment of their journeys over thousands of years and miles to get to your table. I have structured this book for those who are starting at ground zero in the gardening world. I want to present the art of growing vegetables as a complete cycle, not as disjointed tasks.

I have used the terms Old World and New World throughout. The Old World is Europe, Africa, and Asia. The New World is the Americas. These terms have been used since explorers stumbled onto the Americas in the late 1400s. Europeans coined the term New World because, from their point of view, it was new to them. From the perspective of the Indigenous population already living in the Americas, it was not new.

What will you find in this book? Vegetables, of course, but also chapters on soil, location, rotation, definition of terms, and more. You will also find history, planting instructions, and some simple, easy recipes. It is the ability to tie all these aspects together to give you an understanding of how a plant grows, which in turn will give you a harvest.

What tools are needed? Along with the usual shovel, hoe, and rake, you will also need acceptance, curiosity, and patience. The ability to accept that gardening is probably 90% maintenance, i.e., weeding and keeping an eye out for trouble-making insects or diseases. Also, accept that you need to work with nature rather than trying to dominate because nature wins every time. Curiosity to try a new variety, to think through the 'what if I do this' process, which leads to critical thinking. Patience because sometimes what you plant is not what you wanted, it did not survive the season, or all your doubts were for nothing, and you have grown and harvested a beautiful cucumber!

Why would you grow vegetables? For starters, that is not the question. Why wouldn't you grow vegetables is the question. What is the expectation or anticipation that you have looking at a clamshell of strawberries all 12 months compared to the prospect of a local berry farm's seasonal produce or, better yet, in your backyard? There is a difference. That sense of anticipation has been lost with vegetables being available year-round. Here in Washington, we wait for strawberry and asparagus season in the spring. We feast and relish that good summer months are just around the corner.

And the taste! There is less of the original flavor retained the further one gets from the harvest date. It should come as no surprise, therefore, that fresh broccoli tastes better than frozen. Fresh broccoli cut from your garden is even better. It isn't even necessary to peel skin from broccoli stems if just harvested from your garden. It is tender and sweet.

In western Washington, August is the month when my garden reaches its zenith. Yes, I have been harvesting throughout spring, summer and will continue into fall, but the garden bursts in August. I have spent months planning, germinating, planting, transplanting, replanting, snipping, pruning, tying, trellising, caging, fertilizing, watering, weeding, talking to, reasoning with, and even threatening all I can. I stand back and let the garden do what it is programmed to do, realizing that I am part of a process. I am in control of nothing, putting me in my place in the scheme of life, and I am holding on for the ride.

Gardening started eons ago. The first recorded history of gardening is credited to two monks. Both of whom have become patron saints of gardening. The first is Saint Phocas, a Christian monk who lived in the 3rd century AD. He lived outside the village of Sinope in Turkey, growing vegetables to give to the poor. He was persecuted and beheaded in his garden under orders of the district governor for spreading Christian teachings. The second is Saint Fiacre, a Celtic hermit from 7th-century Ireland who eventually immigrated to France and built a hermitage in the village of Seine et Marne for solitude. He spent his time tending to his garden, praying and meditating. This is the rudimentary beginning of monastic gardening. All types of gardens, including vegetable and herb gardens, have evolved from those two.

Vegetable gardens have always been the gardens of the poor, a stepchild to all other gardens.

It can't compare to prima donna rose gardens or unruly gorgeous English cottage perennial gardens. Yet, we couldn't exist without eating plants, whether directly or indirectly. What we know today about vegetables is a culmination of geographic, linguistic, and scientific observations, mutation selection, and just plain curiosity or luck. I would like to bump vegetable gardens up a notch in sophistication and popularity. Welcome, enjoy, and come into my garden.

Chapter 1:
The Mother of All Life

You want to try gardening, but where do you begin? Not by buying seeds or plants but by looking down at your feet. If you don't understand what soil is and its importance, then your gardening results will be baffling.

The terms dirt and soil have a habit of being interchangeable and mean the same thing. They are not interchangeable. There is a huge difference. I grew up calling soil dirt, which, now that I know what the difference is, is quite an insult to soil.

So, what is dirt? It is dislodged soil particles that are no longer part of a functioning environment. Dirt has no identity anymore as far as being part of a unit. It is something you sweep off the kitchen floor, is blown by the wind, it is found under your fingernails and behind a little boy's ears. It is soil that has been torn apart or dismembered. Dirt scientists don't exist.

Soil, on the other hand, is an ecosystem that is under our feet. We just don't see it. Gardeners tend to be concerned about the environment above ground in their gardens. You need to be concerned about the environment below ground. It is more important than a visible one. It is a complete ecosystem of living organisms that live and interact in their surrounding community.

So, along with all other ecosystems that are highly visible, such as rainforests, oceans, prairies, and meadows, now we can add another that we don't see, it is located under our feet and is rarely thought about. Chemicals, oils, or compaction of soil cause harm to productivity, and the results could last for years.

It is dynamic, not static. Soil is always changing due to weathering, so you end up with soils that are in age from young to old. Young soils are the most fertile, but all soils can be brought back to fertility with added amendments and care. Soil is stacked in layers. Think of a layered cake. For our purposes, it is the top layer that is important for growing plants. This top layer is topsoil, and it can be several inches thick to several feet thick.

How do you know the thickness of your topsoil? By digging down until you reach the second layer of soil, which is subsoil. Topsoil will be shades of brown. Think chocolate. Subsoil can be shades of yellow, red, grey/blue, or green blue. Change in color is due to minerals being leached from topsoil or the amount of moisture present. Iron is a common mineral that is leached from the upper soil, and it can give your subsoil a red/orange color. My subsoil is that color. Now you know the thickness of your topsoil, and the thicker, the better.

When you hold a handful of topsoil in your hand, fifty percent of what is in your hand is pore space. Forty-five percent of what is in your hand is rock material, and the remaining five percent is organic material. Remember these percentages.

Pore space in soil has several functions. Where are microbes, bacteria, and animals residing? Enter that fifty percent pore space in your hand. This is the area between rock particles. It is not an empty space but serves as housing for everything living in the soil. We are talking about creatures that are tiny, not visible to the naked eye, and residing in these tiny pore spaces. One teaspoon of topsoil can contain up to one billion organisms. Along with providing housing, it is also the plant's kitchen, allowing microbes, bacteria, vertebrate, and invertebrate animals that reside there to produce a liquid diet that plants need to survive. Nutrients such as calcium, potassium, nitrogen, and phosphorus are broken down chemically to the level of an ion before being utilized by plants. At this point, these nutrients are water-soluble and can be absorbed through a root system.

These pores can fill with water, and controlling water is another function of the fifty percent pore space. Macro and micropore spaces in the soil allow water to either drain away in macro pores or remain in micro pools to be used by plants over a period of time. Both of these activities can occur at the same time. Sand particles and larger rock particles are responsible for creating macro pores. Channels created by earthworms, moles, voles, or even roots also facilitate water to drain. Drainage is critical for flood control and keeping soil from becoming waterlogged but also for leaching harmful or excessive amounts of minerals from topsoil. Silt and clay particles in the soil create micropore spaces that hold water for short periods of time.

Providing space for gas is the third usage for pore spaces in soil. The two life-sustaining gases are carbon dioxide and oxygen. Plants take carbon dioxide from the atmosphere, combining it with water and sunlight to produce sugar. This is photosynthesis. A byproduct of this process is oxygen, which is released to be used by humans and animals. Both of these gases are also present in soil. Organisms in soil need oxygen to survive.

But how did these gases find their way into the soil? There is always an exchange of gases between the atmosphere and soil if conditions are appropriate. Microorganisms, worms, and other creatures that work at decomposing organic material release carbon dioxide and use oxygen. So, for good aeration of the soil, which is the movement of gases in and out of the soil, you need pore spaces. Waterlogged soil or compacted soil do not lend themselves to a good exchange of gases. It becomes oxygen deficient.

Now, on to rock particles that make up the forty-five percent of soil in your hand. Soil comprises three sizes of rock particles: sand, silt, and clay. For a well-balanced soil, a ratio of sand to silt to clay should be percentages of 40:40:20 in that order. Soil with these percentages is termed loam, and this is the balance that everyone strives to achieve. Sand is the size of... well, sand. Silt is smaller than sand and feels similar to flour. Both sand and silt are round. Clay is the smallest and is a flat shape. Silt and clay cannot be seen with the naked eye.

Anyone who lives in a desert environment with only sand knows that water retention is close to zero. It drains away quickly, not leaving enough time for plants to utilize it. A positive attribute of sand is that when mixed with silt or clay, it keeps soil from compacting. It also purifies soil by draining toxic substances.

Silt is the most fertile. Think of the Nile Delta and the agriculture that it has sustained for thousands of years. Silt is found along streams or river beds but is also carried along as a suspended load in river water. Its fertility derives from micro pores that surround silt. These pores hold water and gases for plants to use but also house microbes and bacteria that are essential to healthy soil.

Clay soil is the hardest to work in the garden. Because the individual clay particles are flat, water will lie on the flat surfaces, taking long periods to percolate down. This makes clay feel sticky when wet, and, when dry is difficult to dig. It is great for tennis courts and ceramics. However, a limited amount of clay gives soil body or cohesiveness.

What to do if you have clay soil? Adding sand and organic matter starts a process of changing to a more workable soil. Probably the easiest and quickest method is to build raised beds on top of clay. The depth of a raised bed should be a minimum of 8 inches. If your pocketbook allows, then make it deeper. Either method of adding amendments or a raised bed can be expensive.

Working in clay soil will test anyone's gardening fortitude.

How do you know the percentages of sand, silt, and clay in your soil? There is a general easy test that can give you an answer. Scoop a handful of soil in your hand. It needs to be moist enough to form a ball in the palm of your hand. It should feel similar to silly putty. Work this soil for several minutes until it forms a nice ball. Then, take this ball and squeeze it between your thumb and forefinger. If the soil feels gritty, then it has sand as a major component. If the soil feels rather smooth as flour, then silt is a major component.

How do you know if you have a high clay component? Take a ball of soil and place it between your thumb and forefinger, which are parallel to each other. Push up on the soil ball. You are making a ribbon of soil that will squeeze up and out from your thumb and forefinger. At some point, this ribbon will fall over and break. If the ribbon is only about 1 inch or less in length, then you have about 10% clay. If you can create a ribbon that is 2 inches or longer, then you have around 25% clay. Soils are going to be an endless combination of sand, silt, and clay.

We have covered 95 percent of the soil that is in your hand. The last small, measly five percent is what is going to make or break your gardening adventure. It is organic material. The world's native soils contain roughly five percent organic material. Which is what?

Decayed plant and animal tissue is organic material. It can be created by two methods: composting or humus. The result is the same. Composting is done above ground in concentrated piles or bins. Microbes, bacteria, and other creatures work this material, and it mixes with oxygen, creating heat. I compost my pruning and weeding from the garden, and the following year, I spread it in the garden.

Humus is produced in the soil by microbes, bacteria, and other creatures breaking plant and animal tissue into a plant-usable substance. I take my kitchen scraps to the garden and bury them directly in the garden. Within 2 to 3 months, the buried scraps are gone. Some worry that it will attract rodents, but I have never experienced this.

The word humus is Latin for soil or earth. Our English language has several words that are derived from humus. My favorite is humility. My garden reminds me every summer through my wins and losses that, in the end, I am in control of nothing.

Why is this the most important part of your soil? All creatures that reside in soil or compost piles are dining on this organic smorgasbord and, in turn, feeding plants. You are not feeding your plants, but you are feeding all the creatures in the soil, giving them nourishment and a job to do. Mixing in organic material turns topsoil into 'party central' for biological activity. Both compost and humus are dark in color, having a clean earthy smell.

So, just what is living in your soil? Microbe is a generic term for microfauna and microflora. Animals and plants are small enough that they are only visible under a microscope. One example is nematodes, which are worms, and most are beneficial to your soil. However, there are a few nematodes that are destructive to plant roots. See my chapter on roots. Yeasts, fungi, bacteria, and algae form a short list of microflora. Larger soil-dwelling creatures include snails, slugs, earthworms, beetles, spiders, mice, moles, snakes, and voles. They all have different roles to play. Some are predators preying on and keeping in balance other organisms. Others are consumers whose main function is consuming detritus or dead material. Earthworms, moles, and voles create tunnels that mix soil in small areas, allowing aeration and drainage. Mini rototillers. Earthworms eat their way through soil, munching on dead plant and animal tissue.

And then they poop. Worm poop is called casts, and if there is plant gold in this world, it is worm casts.

What food do these critters live on? Moles feed on worms and other insects. They are responsible for those raised tunnels in the garden. Voles look similar to mice, make holes in the soil, and eat mainly bulbs, roots, and grasses. Insects such as spiders, ants, and beetles eat an assortment of organic material, other insects, and fungi. Earthworms eat dead plant material.

Nematodes eat lawn pests such as ants, fleas, grubs, and termites. Fungi and bacteria are recyclers in soil. They consume soil trash, converting it to nutrients that plants can utilize. They are the workhorses of your soil.

In a natural setting such as a meadow, native plants grow through their yearly life cycle, use nutrients, and they die, decompose, and the nutrients are returned to the soil. A complete cycle. In large-scale farming or gardens, the difference is all or most of the above-ground plant is harvested. It is removed, leaving very little to go back into the soil. Year after year, nutrients are depleted until a point is reached, resulting in sterile soil. This is where commercial fertilizers have saved the day for farmers. It is an artificial replenishment of nutrients bypassing all the organisms living in the soil. There is no middleman.

So… what food can you give your soil critters? This is a brief list of my food sources.

Composted manure. Cow, goat, horse, llama, or chicken manure, when composted, is great for gardens. Do not use fresh manure due to high amounts of nitrogen that may be present. It can burn your plants. It needs to sit for a minimum of six months before using. Composting manure will kill parasites and weed seeds. Do not use cat, dog, or pig manure. Parasites and diseases that may be present in poop from these three can be transmitted to humans.

Bales of straw. I use straw a lot. It is a weed suppressant; it breaks down becoming mulch, helps retain soil moisture, and aids in warming soil in spring. Straw is wheat stalks left after harvesting wheat. Do not use hay. It is a combination of everything that is growing in a field, which includes grasses, weeds, and lots of seeds. You will end up with all sorts of unwanted plants germinating in your garden.

Kitchen scraps. I don't put my kitchen scraps in a compost bin. They are taken to the garden, and I dig a hole, burying them directly. I rotate where it is buried. It takes about 2 or 3 months, and then it is gone. A note of caution: if there is the possibility of a rodent problem, then burying kitchen scraps will invite more trouble.

Fireplace wood ashes. I sprinkle ashes thinly around the garden, and then it is worked into the soil as I weed or plant. Several minerals are present in wood ashes, and they also help keep the acidity/alkaline level of soil in balance.

Green manure. This is adding live plant material back into the soil. Leaving grass clippings on your lawn is adding green manure. I clip vegetable plants to a manageable size, dig a hole, and bury the clippings. Have you ever wondered how a meadow can produce flowers year after year? It is a result of the plants using their own recycled plant material year after year. Plants die, and plant material is slowly broken down, and nutrients are released back into the soil.

Junk mail. I use unwanted paper to line the inside of my garden along the fence line. It is a weed suppressant. It needs to be thick enough to block sunlight. It feeds the worms. I have worms that can read anything.

If you use organic fertilizer such as manures or any other of the previously mentioned ideas, then you are giving the soil microbes and other soil critters something to do, which is decomposing material and creating food for plants. A purpose in life. And it is to your benefit to have all that soil life functioning. If you use non-organic fertilizers, you are bypassing all the soil life and feeding the plant directly. Organic fertilizer will keep your soil healthy and active for the long term. Non-organic fertilizer is a quick fix for plants. The plant is essentially eating a candy bar at 3:30 in the afternoon to get an energy boost. It doesn't last long.

If you use non-organic fertilizer for your plants, then pick one that has the 'big three' nutrients that plants need. These are Nitrogen, Phosphorus, and Potassium. You may need to fertilize several times during the growing season. It does not remain accessible to plants for long periods of time. They are leached out into subsoil.

What to take away from this chapter? First, you need to know how healthy your soil is. Have it tested. Your local Soil Conservation District is a good place to start. Results will show excesses and deficiencies of minerals and nutrients. They will advise how to remedy it.

You have a zoo and plant conservatory existing under your feet. It is a herd or menagerie.

Steven Hawking always encouraged us to look up at the sky. I encourage you to look down at your soil. Just feed it!

Chapter 2:
Locating, Planning, Rotating, Intercropping and Garden Styles

Location, location, location.

Winter is time spent planning a garden. Where to put a garden if just starting out is probably the most critical decision. Whether you have several acres from which to choose, deciding on what spot in the backyard or that south-facing deck if living in an apartment, you need to pick the spot.

A flat sunny area is optimum, which is close to your home, and water is readily accessible.

Vegetables will not grow in shade. Period. Not to contradict myself, but... there are some vegetables that do relatively well in partial or dappled shade. Any of the leaf crops, such as lettuce, spinach, chard, or kale, and root crops do ok. If partial shade is all you have to work with, then try growing them.

If you have a sloping property, then adjust your plans. A gentle south-facing slope will warm faster and is preferable to a north-facing slope. Planting in low areas, such as the base of a hill, is not recommended. The water table might be close to the surface, creating drainage problems.

Also, low areas are last to warm during the daytime. Cold air accumulates in low areas that might be subject to frosts.

Wherever you put your garden, it should be the sunniest and warmest area. Vegetables need full sun for a minimum of 6 to 8 hours. Think about the sun and shade patterns in the designated area that you will be using. If you have plants that provide shade, then you might consider removing some or all. There is nothing wrong with taking out a tree or shrub that you may not be in love with and would be happy to see gone.

Planning.

Once you have selected a site for your garden, then other doors open for planning. Fencing, size, types of gardens, and amount of time you want to dedicate. These all factor into creating a garden.

Should you fence your garden? If you are planning to establish a garden in an open area some distance from your house and don't want to chase deer, rabbits, woodchucks, raccoons, skunks, opossums, or any other visitor that happens to reside in your area, then a fence is for you.

However, it is not a fail-proof solution, but it works most of the time. Some determined animals may still jump over, dig under, or climb over fencing. My garden is fenced with 6-foot-2-inch mesh fencing. I did not bury a foot of fencing in the ground to ward off those that burrow, and as of this writing, I do not have a problem. Hopefully, I have not just jinxed myself.

However, I stood in the garden and watched a juvenile rabbit squeeze through my fence to escape. Now what? My solution is bird netting. It is inexpensive and lasts. I cut strips that are 3 feet wide, attaching them to the outside of the fence. This netting covers fencing well over 2 feet high, leaving a good 3 to 4 inches of netting on the ground. Normally, animals don't like walking on it, but sometimes get tangled on it. I use ordinary twist ties for attaching. It is not rocket science, but it has kept young rabbits out.

Size is also important. If this is a new adventure, then start small. Can anything be more frustrating than opting in for something too big to handle? How about a four-by-four-foot area or several containers? You can always expand. Will any family members be helping, or is this your hobby alone? Start with some easy vegetables to grow that your family will actually eat, planting a small variety. Lettuce, carrots, radishes, and peas would be good choices. Plant a cherry tomato. There isn't anything more satisfying than plucking and snacking on a cherry tomato that you grew.

Location and size will dictate how you garden. Did you know that there are different types of models for planting? It opens up all sorts of possibilities for physical limitations and the amount of time dedicated to gardening.

Turning over a piece of your property for planting is the standard. For an 'in-ground' garden, removal of existing grass or vegetation is a must. If the area is small enough, this can be accomplished by digging out the vegetation or by laying sheets of cardboard down in the fall. The good news is the cardboard will break down and become compost. This will allow enough time for the existing plant material to die before spring. Just don't use waxed cardboard. If a garden is big enough, you may have to use a tractor to scrape the vegetation.

Intensive gardening is great for backyards with limited space. Historically, gardens have been laid out in neat rows with a lot of wasted space in between. Intensive gardening does away with wasted space. An example of intensive gardens is square-foot gardening. It is simply partitioning into square foot areas. For all those closet engineers out there, this could be the method for you. It will be designed, planned, and organized to your heart's content or as your time and maintenance allow.

Plants that are good candidates for square-foot gardens are lettuce, carrots, radishes, beets, chard, spinach, Brussels sprouts, onions, basil, parsley, chives, peppers, eggplant, or garlic.

Vegetables that I would not plant in a square foot area are squash, tomatoes, beans, potatoes, corn, or cabbages. These plants, if grown in fertile soil, could reach sizes that are too big for a one-foot square area and would take over adjacent areas. Planting in close proximity requires an additional amount of nutrients and moisture. Soil with adequate organic matter is a must. You can find layout designs for square-foot gardens in books and online.

Vertical planting is on trellises, poles, cages, nets, fencing, or anything else you can create for support. Your plants will grow up and not out, which means there is less bending and less ground space used. You just need to think three-dimensional. Vegetable options for vertical planting are pole beans, pole peas, tomatoes, melons, cucumbers, and squash. Place vertically growing plants on the north side of your garden; they will capture the sun but will not shade everything else.

Constructing a raised bed is another arrangement. It will sit on top of your existing lawn without digging and have the added bonus of less weeding and maintenance. Notice I said less weeding. The myth of no weeding is just that. Laying sheets of cardboard to cover the garden site starts the process. This helps keep grass from growing up through your raised bed. Next, you need to decide what material to use for the frame of the bed. Some good choices are rot-resistant wood such as cedar, redwood, white oak, or Douglas fir. Rot resistance means just that. It will eventually break down but at a much slower pace than other woods. Never, ever, use treated lumber or railroad ties. The chemicals in these products eventually leach out, find their way into the soil, and can be absorbed by vegetables. Using concrete blocks, stone, or bricks for a frame is another option.

How big should a raised bed be? Width 'should be so contrived that the hands of those who weed them may easily reach the middle of their breadth.'* That was written in 1594 and is still good advice today, usually around 3 feet wide. Length can be as long as you want. The object is not to have to walk in a raised bed. Now, you are ready to fill your frame with soil. Buy soil from a reputable nursery or landscape business. Using fill dirt should not be an option. It usually has all sorts of foreign items in it and probably will not be a good, healthy, fertile medium for your vegetables. Soil depth should be at least 8 inches for shallow-rooted vegetables such as lettuce and some carrot varieties. If you plan to plant cucumbers, beans, or tomatoes, then you need at least 10 to 12 inches deep to allow adequate root growing room. Mulching is highly recommended. Raised beds dry faster than in-ground planting, and mulch helps keep moisture in the soil.

Container gardening is a simple solution for small areas or utilizing a porch or deck with sun. Whatever type of container you use, it needs to have drainage holes. Your efforts will end in failure otherwise. Soil needs to be a light soil, meaning it should be porous enough for water and air circulation. Garden soil may be too heavy. Also, bear in mind that soil in containers will dry out faster and will be leached of nutrients faster. Watering may need to be done daily on hot days. Fertilizing needs to be done more often. If you are using a potting medium that has fertilizer incorporated, then you are good for about 8 weeks. After that, you should add a water-soluble fertilizer or slow-release fertilizer every three weeks. These are synthetic fertilizers, and they work well in containers. Follow instructions and don't over-fertilize because roots can be burned from too much fertilizing, and the plant will die.

So, you want to try a tomato in a pot. What size do you need? Something that is a 5-gallon pot or at least 2 feet in diameter and at least 2 feet deep. The bigger, the better. It could be a pretty pot but also a 5-gallon bucket or a bushel basket; just use your imagination and make sure you have enough drainage holes in the bottom. Another option is a grow bag. These are cloth bags, reusable if kept dry over winter, and come in different sizes for different plants. Cherry tomatoes or bush tomatoes work well in containers. Planting a tomato start is the same whether you are planting in a container or in the ground. Pinch off the bottom two leaves. Plant tomatoes deep enough to cover the stem area where the bottom two leaves were removed. Tomatoes have nodes on their stems that will develop into roots, so you will have a sturdier plant by planting it deep.

One last option. Ripping out parts of an existing flower bed and converting to vegetables. I know this is sacrilegious to some. Just think outside the box. I have removed perennials from a bed and converted it into an edible landscape. I cannot physically keep up with it, and I am no longer interested in it. I kept dahlias, peonies, and lilies, which the deer seem to leave alone. One vegetable that is now in the old flower bed is artichoke. Artichokes are a perennial vegetable, and the shape and texture of artichoke plants add an interesting element to the bed. A deer-proof perennial, and we get to eat artichokes. You are mixing ornamental plants with vegetables.

I encourage you to investigate and determine what might work best for you. I also encourage you, when doing your research, to look at the edu sites, reputable seed company websites, or reputable garden sites. Stay away from some .com sites. The edu sites and seed company sites are based on research, and the .com sites can be based on selling a product, pseudoscience, wives' tales, or any other nonsense.

Rotating.

Rotation of vegetables is critical to maintaining the sustainable health of your soil. It just means moving the plants to different locations every 1 to 3 years. In small raised beds, rotation is probably not an option, but a way to handle rotation is to plant completely different vegetables every year. Learn the family members of your favorite vegetables because planting vegetables year after year that are in the same family will not help your soil. An example is the Solanaceae or nightshade family. Tomato, potato, eggplant, and pepper, to name a few, are in the Solanaceae family. If you planted tomatoes in your raised bed one year, then the next year, plant vegetables from another family such as Brassicaceae or cabbage family. These would include cabbage, broccoli, cauliflower, and kale, to name a few. So you are trading tomatoes for broccoli. Can't give up planting tomatoes every year? Try growing tomatoes in large pots. So, you give your garden soil a break from tomatoes but still have tomatoes to munch on.

Grow bags are another option for above-ground planting. Some years, I plant potatoes in grow bags. Every year, I fill the bags with new soil, and this allows me to keep the potatoes in the same vicinity or spot. After harvesting the potatoes in the fall, the soil in the bags is spread around in the garden. One word of caution. If your potatoes develop diseases during the growing season, I would opt out of spreading the soil in the garden.

Different crops use nutrients in varying amounts. Rotation of vegetables reduces the risk of depleting soil of a particular nutrient. It helps keep soil fertility balanced. Moving legumes to a different spot every year helps with nitrogen replenishment in the soil. I plant several varieties of peas and beans in small plots, and the following year they are planted in a new area.

Rotation also helps keep food sources and habitat to a minimum for insect pests and holds down soil diseases.

A good example of an insect pest, its food source, and its habitat is the tomato hornworm. A hornworm can be several different shades of green, so they are somewhat camouflaged on a tomato leaf. They are large caterpillars, sometimes having white 'v-shaped' markings on the body. It gets its name because, on the last abdomen section, there is a black horn-shaped protrusion. They defoliate the leaves and small stems. It has one or two generations per year, depending on the region, and spends the winter as pupae in the soil. The pupae stage is between the larval or egg stage and adulthood. In the spring, an adult hornworm develops from the pupae and exits the soil as a hawk or sphinx moth. This is a big moth with a wingspan of 4 inches. The top side of the abdomen has 5 yellow spots down each side and ends in a point. Adults hover over flowers, taking nectar, usually in the evening. The adult moths mate, and the female lays eggs on the tomato leaf. The eggs hatch in 4 to 5 days, and the caterpillars begin eating your tomato plant. After they have reached full size, they migrate down to the soil and change into pupae. So, the moth has a convenient plant to lay eggs and a ready-made meal for the growing offspring. If I find them, I just collect them and send them to hornworm heaven, and I move my plants around every year, so hopefully there are no hornworm pupae in the new area soil.

Pathogens in the soil that depend on certain plants for nutrients tend to build up in the soil over years if the same plant is repeatedly planted in the same place. You could end up with soil that you may need to leave fallow or empty for several years due to high levels of pathogens. The easiest way around this potential problem is to move the crops around. You have to remember that soils are alive, and they can become depleted of nutrients or have an overabundance of a pathogen. This results in a sick soil.

Intercropping.

What is intercropping, and why would you do it? It is simply planting two or more different plants in close proximity that co-exist and is sometimes referred to as companion planting. There are several benefits to this practice. Economy of using garden space is one. Combining horizontal ground-level space with vertical space. An example is trellising peas and planting lettuce or carrots at the base of peas. Pole beans with spinach, radishes, or lettuce. Bush beans with staked tomatoes. Planting corn and zucchini together. Corn is tall and straight up, while zucchini is low and meandering. Brussels sprouts, which grow up to 2 feet tall, and radishes, which have a height of 3 or 4 inches, go together well. Different above-ground growth patterns can add eye appeal to a garden. Think of three dimensions.

Planting different vegetables with different root systems is another example of intercropping. Different root depths and different root patterns. Roots from different plants will not compete for the same area. Depth of roots is categorized as shallow, medium, or deep. Examples of shallow depth, which is 6 to 18 inches, are the cabbage family, potatoes, onions, leeks, lettuce, and spinach. Medium depth of 18 to 24 inches. Examples are peppers, carrots, eggplants, rutabagas, and cucumbers. Deep roots go 24 inches and more. Artichokes, parsnips, tomatoes, asparagus, corn, and pumpkins are in this category. So, planting a cabbage next to a tomato is a good combination. Carrots and lettuce together because carrots have a main large tap root, and lettuce has a small tap root with lateral roots that have a shallow spread. They don't compete for the same space.

Another method is planting different vegetables that mature at different times. There are short-season crops and long-season crops. Vegetables have a variety of days to maturity, from 30 days to 120 days. Planting arugula, which matures in 40 days around a cabbage seedling. The cabbage seedling will take 90 days or more before it is ready to harvest. So, the arugula is harvested before the large cabbage leaves spread and cover the arugula. Tomatoes with chard. Tomatoes are ready in around 4 months, and chard is ready in 2 months or less.

Another benefit is shading during the summer months. Cucumbers and lettuce. If growing cucumbers vertically, then they provide shade on their north side, and lettuce will thrive in the shade of cucumbers during warm summer months. Cucumbers produce a small microclimate for the lettuce to survive in warm months. Pole beans and spinach are another happy couple.

Who wouldn't want a plant that suppresses weeds? Well, planting nasturtiums around your tomatoes will help keep weeds away. It smothers the ground with leaves and flowers, not letting anything else grow. And it adds color to your garden.

Probably the most famous of intercropping is the Three Sisters. Corn, squash, and beans. Corn offers support for beans, whereas beans put nitrogen back into the soil. Squash offers shade at the base of corn and beans, which helps hold moisture in the soil, but also, the spiny leaves deter small animals from nibbling on the corn and bean stocks. It is a perfect threesome.

This is an incomplete list of intercropping or companion plants. What are their attributes? Economy of space, non-competitive roots, different harvesting times, providing micro shade areas, and weed control. So plant your garden in onesies and practice polyculture. It makes gardens more interesting to explore and healthier.

One final thought on intercropping plants. Plants do not have the ability to protect a neighboring plant from destructive insects. They also do not have the ability to 'love' another plant. The kindest response to this idea is that it is nothing more than attributing a human emotion, love to a plant. It is a silly, ridiculous theory. What plants do have is the ability, through flowers or emitting scents, to attract certain insects that will, in turn, attack destructive insects.

The intermingling of plants has been done since Medieval times. So the Medieval English garden that we have idyllic images of was a compilation of a little bit of everything edible and, in some cases, non-edible. The Medieval herbs were divided between kitchen and infirmary or medicinal herbs. Plants utilized included vegetables, fruits, grasses, flowers, and roots. Gardening has changed through the years, and, for small gardens, I am not sure it has been a progression.

Monoculture, which is planting all tomatoes together, all lettuce together, etc., invites trouble. Scattering your plantings doesn't give pests a large target, and areas will not be totally depleted of specific nutrients. It gives a garden eye appeal, texture, and invites someone to walk through a garden, discovering what is planted. And DON'T spray your herbs for diseases or pests if you are using herbs for culinary purposes.

*Landsberg, Sylvia. The Medieval Garden. Principles of Measurement and Layout. Page 91.

Chapter 3:
Floral Arrangements

Putting flowers in my vegetable garden started out as an act of necessity. I rescued some plants in the unfenced front of our property from deer. And from this, I realized that flowers scattered throughout the vegetable garden added color, contrast, an invitation for pollinators, and, in some cases, scents to the garden. There was no looking back.

Nasturtium.

Nasturtium has been in our gardens for hundreds of years to the point of being ignored and overlooked for new and exciting flowers. Well, let's look again. It requires very little care and very little fertilizer, and will thrive even in poor soil.

It is an annual, but in some zones, a perennial New World plant with a region of origin in South and Central America. It is in the Tropaeotaceae family that includes only one genus but 80 different species, and is a very distant cousin of cabbage. Leaves, flowers, and seeds are edible. Incas dined on them. Taste is somewhat peppery, similar to Nasturtium officinale, which is watercress. Not only was the taste similar, but it took its common name of nasturtium from watercress. The word has its origin in Latin 'nas' for nose and 'tortum' for twist. Tasting made your nose wrinkle.

How does nasturtium help your garden? It can be a bait trap for aphids and white cabbage butterflies. These insects prefer a nasturtium over a member of the cabbage family. If you find aphids or white cabbage butterfly eggs on your nasturtium, just pluck the infested leaves or any other part of the plant and dispose of it. It also suppresses weeds and holds moisture in the soil by covering the ground with its leaves. The flowers are large and produce exceedingly sweet nectar that hummingbirds love. The shape of the flower makes a perfect landing spot for bees to settle to collect pollen and nectar. And it happily reseeds itself the following year. Seeds are large and resemble garbanzos.

Varieties today are many, and it is a child-friendly seed to plant. Seeds are big enough for small hands to handle and will germinate in 7 to 14 days. They need to be planted 1 inch deep and require darkness to germinate. They are happy in lightly fertilized soil, grow quickly, and will continue to bloom all summer. Pluck some flower petals that are not resting on the ground, don't wash them, and add them to a salad just before serving after the dressing. A burst of color in a salad and your garden. Nasturtiums are deer-resistant most of the time.

Marigold.

This is one annual flower that probably is in everyone's garden. It is a New World plant in the Asteraceae/Compositae or sunflower family, along with asters, daisies, sunflowers, and dandelions. Its place of origin is in Mexico and Guatemala. It was brought to Europe in the late 1500s, and the Spanish placed the flowers at the altar of the Virgin Mary. They were called 'Mary's Gold,' which eventually morphed into marigolds.

There are two varieties of marigolds: the French marigold and the African marigold. The French variety is short, usually no more than 16 inches, with flowers that are similar to a daisy configuration, while the African variety is tall, up to two feet, with flowers that have a pom-pom configuration. Both are deer-resistant and attract butterflies. Seeds were brought back from Central America by Spanish explorers and eventually found their way to France. The French adopted and cultivated new varieties. Seeds from France migrated to northern Africa and naturalized. Marigolds found their way to North America in the late 1700s.

Non-ornamental uses for marigolds are many. In Mexico and Guatemala, it is known as Flor de Muerto and placed on graves celebrating All Souls Day. One of the most popular flowers in India, they are used in weddings and decorating temples. Flower petals are edible, but some varieties do not have a pleasant taste. Those that do have a pleasant taste are a colorful addition to any salad, known also as the poor man's saffron. Do some research on different varieties that are recommended for consumption based on taste. It is also added to chicken feed to enhance the yolk color.

This is another plant that is not too fussy with growing requirements. Heat and drought tolerant, they are happy in fertile, loamy soil with sun. I start seeds indoors, and plants are transplanted after the last frost date. They are happy blooming all summer into fall.

Do marigolds repel pests, or do they attract beneficial insects that then dine on the insect pests?

Research has found that they do the latter. Lady bugs and parasitic wasps are drawn to marigolds. Roots produce a chemical that may inhibit nematode eggs from hatching in the soil. It is the following year that you may see the results of this because there will not be a new generation of nematodes in your soil. So plant marigolds, and then the following year, plant carrots or tomatoes on that same spot. This is a multipurpose plant that is easy to grow and low maintenance once it is established.

Borage.

Borage or starflower is an herb that I insert among the flowers. It is an Old World annual native to the Mediterranean region and is in the Boraginaceae family. It is sometimes placed in the weed section because it reseeds itself very easily and will grow almost anywhere. Garbage piles, junk yards, roadside ditches, it really isn't picky. It reaches a height of 3 feet with hairy leaves and stems and beautiful blue star-shaped flowers.

Eating borage was thought to give courage and be an antidepressant in ancient Roman times. In medieval England, borage leaves were infused in wines or clarets to give the drinker a sense of well-being or courage. Today, the oil derived from borage seeds is sold as a GLA supplement. This supplement could reduce inflammation. Other benefits have been reported but are scientifically unsubstantiated. Flowers and leaves are edible, adding a cucumber taste to your salad. Flowers can be frozen in ice cubes for a festive drink. Removing the hairy sepal to eat the flower is simple. Hold the flower stem with one hand and gently pinch and pull the flower away from the stem. It will pop right off.

Flowers are a seduction for bees. They swarm the plant. It can also provide habitat for lacewings. Hummingbirds and parasitic wasps will also flock to the flowers. Seeds germinate in two weeks or less, need full sun, and will even grow in poor soil. After the first year, if left to go through the full cycle, then the plants will happily reseed for years to come.

Another quality that is attributed to borage is a dynamic accumulator. Which means what? For years, some plants have had the reputation of the ability to gather trace minerals and nutrients from soil. It is absorbed through roots and transferred to leaves. At the end of the growing season, these plants are composted and worked back into the soil. This adds additional amounts of minerals and nutrients back for next year's plant growth. Not enough research has been done to substantiate this process, but composting any healthy plant material from your garden is beneficial.

Sow seeds ½ inch deep after the last frost date. Germination takes place between 5 and 15 days. It is happy in full sun or partial shade, drought tolerant after it is established, reaches 2 to 3 feet tall, and, best of all, it is deer resistant. Seed life is 3 years, but honestly, if it flowers and goes to seed, you will never have to replant.

So planting borage will give you lots of bees among other pollinators in your garden, pretty star-shaped blue flowers, edible leaves and flowers with a cucumber taste, low maintenance, happy to reseed itself, and a good composting plant. And some still classify borage as a weed! A very beneficial weed indeed.

Alyssum.

A native to southern Europe, northern Africa, and Eurasia, it is a low-mounding plant reaching only 5 or 6 inches tall and grown as an annual or perennial. It is in the Brassicaceae or cabbage family and has been around since the 1500s. The name Alyssum comes from the Greek Allyson, meaning 'without madness,' and was believed to cure rabies. Flowers and leaves are edible. This is another plant that will happily reseed itself for the following year.

It is heat tolerant and soil tolerant as long as there is good drainage and moderate moisture, but can tolerate some drought. In other words, it is not a picky plant to have in your garden. It will grow between rocks, is great in borders or containers, and will be happy in sun or partial shade. It can carpet an area in the garden with fragrant tiny flowers in a range of colors that will attract bees. Hoverflies and parasitic wasps are also attracted to Alyssum, and as stated earlier, these good insects help keep the bad insects under control.

Fuchsia.

Most fuchsias are native to Central and South America. In the late 1600s, Charles Plumier, a French monk and botanist, is credited with naming and describing the first fuchsia, which he found in Hispaniola. He named it after a German botanist, Leonhart Fuchs, who lived in the 1500s.

Fuchsia is in the Onagraceae or evening primrose family of plants, which are found on every continent. Most members are classified in the wildflower or weed section. Some examples, along with fuchsias, are suncups, evening primrose, fireweed, and pink fairies. Most fuchsias are considered tropical shrubs, but some have a trailing growth habit, which makes them a good candidate for hanging baskets. Fuchsias are either 'tender' or 'hardy.' Tender fuchsias are annuals and will not survive the winter. Hardy fuchsias are perennials that will survive the winter.

All flowers have four main parts, which are sepals, petals, pistils, and stamen. Some plants present these parts in interesting arrangements, and fuchsia is an excellent example. The configuration of these parts draws gardeners to collect different fuchsias. It is also a favorite of hummingbirds. The classic teardrop shape starts at a junction on a plant stem where there is a stalk known as a pedicel. This pedicel is a short stalk or stem. Attached to the pedicel is a small tube-shaped part. This is the ovary where seeds develop. Next will be the sepals. Generally, sepals will be green-leaf-shaped, but in the case of fuchsias, the sepals are long and slender in vibrant colors. The purpose of sepals is to encapsulate the immature flower bud.

Next are the petals, which are modified leaves. Fuchsias have a range of petal numbers. A single fuchsia has four petals, a semi-double has between five to seven petals, and a double has eight or more, all of them resembling miniature skirts. The collective name for all the petals is corolla. The function of the corolla is to protect the inner reproductive parts of the flower but also to attract pollinators. Corollas have developed a range of colors and, in some cases, scents to attract pollinators. The flower feeds the pollinator with nectar, and the pollinator spreads pollen within the individual flower or adjacent flowers to fertilize. Everyone benefits.

Enclosed by the corolla are the reproductive parts of the flower. The female reproductive part is the pistil. It has three components. First is the ovary, which, in the case of fuchsia, is the small tube attached to the pedicel. What you see next at the base of the corolla is the style and stigma. The style is one long filament, and the stigma is a sticky small bulb shape at the end of the style. It is sticky to collect pollen from the pollinators.

The male reproductive part is the stamen, and fuchsias have eight stamens that hang down along with the pistil. These eight filaments are shorter in length than the pistil and also have a swollen bulb at the end, which contains the pollen. Both the eight stamens and one pistil are attached to the ovary. They both hang through the corolla and exit at the bottom of the corolla. They are very visible, and the whole flower resembles a miniature wind chime.

The attraction of hummingbirds to fuchsias is due to a range of reasons. The color of flowers, which tend to be in the red range, catches their attention. The teardrop or tubular shape is a good match to their long, narrow bill and tongue. Because flowers hang down, it is easy for hummingbirds to hover collecting the nectar. But the flowers also get something from this relationship. While the birds are hovering, they brush against the stamens, getting pollen on their foreheads, which then gets deposited on the sticky stigma.

So the result is fuchsia flowers are pollinated, and hummingbirds dine on sweet nectar. Having several hardy fuchsias in your garden is a magnet for hummingbirds and helps them on their migratory journey.

Milkweed.

Milkweed is in the Apocynaceae or dogbane family. Periwinkle and oleander, along with milkweed, are some familiar plants in this family. Milkweed is native to North America, a perennial, and it is another plant that humans have relegated to the weed section. They will grow almost anywhere. Open fields, roadside ditches, wet areas, and your garden. For Monarch butterflies, it is their host plant and lifeline. These butterflies have recently been moved to the endangered species list due to their declining numbers.

Adult Monarchs feed on flower nectar of several plants, including milkweed, but they only lay eggs on milkweed. The life cycle of a Monarch is only 2 to 5 weeks during the breeding season. An adult will breed and deposit eggs on milkweed. The eggs hatch after 3 to 5 days, and they develop into caterpillars that feed on the leaves. Caterpillars live 11 to 18 days, and then they develop into a chrysalis. This is a transition phase from caterpillar to butterfly. The caterpillar will develop a hard outer casing and will transform itself into a butterfly. This takes about two weeks. The butterfly breaks out of the hard shell, and a new generation is ready to repeat the process of migrating further north. So the Monarch that leaves Mexico or California never lives long enough to reach their summer destinations, and it is a hopscotch of three or four generations of Monarchs that travel north. The last generation to mature will return to Mexico or California without breeding, flying 2000 to 3000 miles to overwinter. This generation can live up to 9 months before starting the annual trip north in the spring. So, it is critical for the caterpillar stage of Monarchs to have a food source waiting for them on their migration.

A milky latex substance found in the tissue cells of milkweed gives it its name. Cardiac glycoside is a heart poison to humans and animals. Monarch caterpillars can dine on it without any adverse reactions. Who else benefits from milkweed? Indigenous Americans have used it for centuries for different medicinal purposes. Another interesting product is the white floss that is inside the seed pod attached to the brown seeds. This floss is very buoyant, repelling water, and was used extensively during WWII to stuff life jackets. It is also a good natural stuffing material for pillows and mattresses and a natural source for insulating clothing. Humans have eaten different parts of the plant depending on various growth stages. Specific cooking instructions are a must to remove the poisons. I leave eating milkweed to the Monarchs to enjoy.

Growing milkweed is easy; once it is established in full sun, it will grow even in poor soil. It develops deep roots, so it does not do well being transplanted. Height varies from 2 to 6 feet on sturdy stems, so staking isn't necessary. In late fall, I cut mine back to the ground, and they pop up again in the spring. If you let the seed pods mature and they burst open, then the plant happily reseeds the area with new young plants. Deer leave it alone, and I use milkweed as a 'guard' plant to surround other plants that the deer will eat. It is not 100% effective, but it helps.

There are varieties of milkweed for every region, and I encourage you to grow the variety that is specific to your area. A good website that guides you to the right variety is

https://www.xerces.org/milkweed/milkweed-guides.

A good guide to finding the right seed source for your region is https://xerces.org/milkweed/milkweed-seed-finder. Monarchs need our help, and we can do this.

Chapter 4: Cabbage Big and Small

Cabbage

Cabbage belongs to a huge family of edible and non-edible plants with two names and a long history to confuse us all. Why, oh why, would it have two names to confuse us? It was known as Cruciferae up until the 20th Century. Crucifer is Latin for cross, which describes the arrangement of flower petals for all plants in this family. Then, around 1980, scientists decided to change the name to Brassicaceae. Brassica is Latin, which is from the Celtic 'bresic,' which means cabbage. So, the common name for this family is now the cabbage family. This puts more emphasis on the plants that are edible.

Cabbage's ancestor is an Old World plant that is thought to have originated in Eastern Europe. Wild cabbage or sea cabbage looks similar to mustard or collard, grows along coastlines, is a perennial, and does not form a head. It can still be found growing along the coastlines of Great Britain, northern Europe, and the north coast of the Mediterranean. Romans had a love of cabbages, using them as food but also medicinally.

Eating cabbages was believed to ward off hangovers and act as a laxative. Between the Roman and Renaissance periods, cabbages became associated with peasantry. They were relegated to being a poor relative of the vegetable world. "Rustic" was a kind and generous descriptive adjective for cabbage, and it has been associated with the lower economic class throughout history. English peasants in the Middle Ages had a small range of vegetables comprising cabbages, onions, and leeks day in and day out, with dried peas or beans breaking up the monotony of their diet. Let's see if we can improve its status.

I don't think there is another vegetable that has gone from a wild ancestor to such a wide range of cultivated forms as cabbage. This wild plant has been domesticated to give us Brussels sprouts, cauliflower, broccoli, kale, mustard, kohlrabi and cabbage. They are all cabbages; they just look different.

Possibly the oldest of cultivated vegetables, cabbages were known as Cole crops. The word 'cole' comes from the Latin 'caulis,' which means stem. Cabbages long ago were eaten for their stems.

Cultivation and spread of cabbage is given to the Celts who inhabited central Europe. They really liked their cabbages. So, some form of primitive-headed cabbage has been consumed from ancient Celtic times through the Roman, Middle Ages, Renaissance Italy, and Medieval England. Arabs who conquered large swaths of Europe during the Middle Ages settled in those conquered lands and brought with them new agricultural innovations that improved cabbage varieties. Cabbage was brought to Canada by Jacques Cartier in the mid-1500s and, from there, spread south to the American colonies. And it continued to evolve, with most new varieties coming from Northern Europe.

The term 'colewort' is a Medieval English word and refers to cabbage that did not form a head. Today's examples would be collard, mustard, or kale. The word 'cabbage' comes to us from the Middle English 'caboge,' which came from Old North French 'caboche.' Caboche is traced back to the Latin 'caput,' meaning head. Cabbage is also meant to steal or to filch. This plant has had a hard road to any sophistication. Our term 'coleslaw' is derived from the Dutch word 'koolsla' which means cabbage salad.

Cabbage that forms a head is referred to as hardheaded cabbage and was developed in the cooler regions of Northern Europe. It has tightly spaced leaves on a truncated or shortened stem. These leaves can be smooth or wrinkled with colors ranging from white, green, purple, and red. It is a biennial, but gardeners treat it as an annual. Planting to harvest takes place in one year.

After a cabbage has been harvested and if the plant remains in the ground, then two events take place. First, the cabbage plant will develop side shoots of smaller cabbages that can be harvested. These might have the appearance of Brussels sprouts, only larger. Then, in its second year, it will produce a stalk and will flower. Bees love these yellow flowers.

Seeds are the size of poppy seeds. It never ceases to amaze me that something that small will grow into a huge cabbage with all the supporting leaves in 3 to 5 months. Not only is there a lot of genetic information packed into that tiny seed, but also a lunch box with enough nutrition for seeds to germinate and start growing. I germinate seeds indoors in small pots, putting three or four seeds into each pot. Moisten soil before planting, scatter seeds on top of rough soil, add a dusting of more soil on top, and gently pat to smooth the surface. These seeds are so small they will fall down between soil particles and will be deep enough to germinate and start growing. I lay a piece of kitchen plastic wrap over the pots, which acts as a simple greenhouse. There usually is no need to water again until seeds have sprouted and are growing. In my region, I start seeds in February and then, in March, move them out to a portable greenhouse.

Seeds can also be directly sowed in the garden ¼ inch deep. My reason for starting seeds indoors is to control soil temperature for germination. It needs to be around 75F. If direct sowing in the garden, then you may have to wait a few weeks. Cabbage is a cool weather crop, so in my region, I start in February or March but also in July or early August for a fall crop. Check your local extension office for growing details in your area.

Plants will pop up after a week or so. When they are 4 to 6 weeks old and have developed two true leaves, then they can be transplanted outdoors. Young plants cannot survive a hard frost. If you are in a region that gets consistent hard frosts in spring, then hold off planting for a while.

Cabbages planted for a fall harvest that are well established can survive early fall frosts. In milder regions, cabbages can survive winter with some protection. Winter gardening is always a gamble but worth the try.

Days to maturity or harvest range from 65 to 100 days, depending on variety. Cabbage does best when the air temperature is between 55F to 75F in a sunny location. They need to be watered evenly through the growing season and are heavy feeders. What does that mean? Don't let them dry out for long periods of time, but also don't water so much that there is standing water. Fertilizing is done when the seedlings are first planted and then again halfway through the growing season. I use composted manure both times, working it into the soil. The plants stand a better chance of being fed consistently over the growing season using organic fertilizer. Cabbage seeds remain viable for 5 years if kept in a cool, dry place. Trying new varieties every year can lead to new favorites.

My major cabbage pest is the cabbage worm. You may notice a small white moth flying in your garden in early spring. There are no flowers at this time of year, so it is not looking for nectar. This is an adult cabbage worm looking for a cabbage leaf to lay a single tiny egg. After the egg hatches, you start seeing a green, velvety-looking caterpillar on your leaves. They eat irregularly shaped holes in cabbage leaves, and when I find them, I pick and squish them.

Another problem I have encountered is a head of cabbage that has cracked. Fall rain in our region is the culprit. Too much rain with temperature fluctuations will cause leaves to burst and crack. Every season is different, and you need to watch the weather, deciding when to harvest.

Every region comes with its own list of pests and diseases due to different climates. Become good friends with your local extension office. There is a wealth of information out there.

Cabbage is a good source of vitamin C, K, and manganese. Ships setting out in the 1700s took crates of cabbages to prevent scurvy which is caused by a deficiency of vitamin C. Fermented cabbage, such as sauerkraut and kimchi, have lots of probiotics. These nourish good bacteria in your stomach, which in turn helps keep you healthy and your digestive tract working correctly.

Chemicals present in cabbage have anti-inflammatory properties. Leaves have been used as compresses for external wounds. It is the sulfur contained in leaves that heals wounds but also makes your kitchen stink from overcooking cabbage. You get the most bang for your buck when you eat cabbage raw or fermented.

Premium Late Dutch cabbage is one of my standard cabbages. It is a round, smooth-leafed green cabbage with a flat top and bottom. Introduced to North America by German immigrants in the 1860s, it can weigh 10 to 15 pounds. Leaves are large, not as thick as other cabbages, and are not as tightly spaced, which makes for easy removal. This cabbage is a good candidate for cabbage rolls. Days to maturity are around 100, so it is considered a late-season variety and stores well over winter. I store cabbages on a table in the garage. It is a cool, dark area, and cabbages will last until about March before they start to look a little sad.

Brunswick is another standard cabbage for me. It is a round or drumhead smooth-leafed green cabbage. It is a good workhorse cabbage good for just about anything from kraut, stir fry, or coleslaw. It is another German introduction from the 1920s. Leaves are tightly spaced, and this cabbage can reach the size of a cannonball. It matures in 90 days and is very cold hardy. It also stores well over winter.

Violaceo de Verona is a drop-dead gorgeous round heirloom green and purple cabbage. I don't think you can call many cabbages drop-dead gorgeous, but this one is. It is a savoy-type cabbage, which means the leaves are wrinkled and not smooth. Originated, as its name implies, in the Verona region of Italy. Matures in 100 days. Cold, hardy, with excellent sweet flavor.

Tete Noire is a smooth, leaved, deep dark purple cabbage from France. It matures in 60 days with sweet, crunchy leaves. Red or purple color is confined to the outer layer of cells. So when you cut through a purple cabbage leaf, the cells in the middle will be white or green. Purple cabbages have a higher amount of antioxidants than green cabbages, which helps keep our cardiovascular system healthy.

Another shape for cabbages is pointed or conical.

One of my favorites is **Kalibos**. Considering a cabbage in the realm of sensuality may seem an oxymoron, but if there will ever be a sensual cabbage, then it is Kalibos. It is conical in shape, wider at the hips, and tapering to a point on top. Purple smooth leaves are tight, gracefully swirl, and embrace each other as if doing a tango. It matures in 85 days and can weigh from 2 to 3 pounds. It is an heirloom from Eastern Europe.

Early Jersey Wakefield cabbage developed from Early Wakefield cabbage, which found its way to North America from Yorkshire, England, in the 1840s. German gardeners tried growing the Early Wakefield in New Jersey, but the climate and soil were not beneficial. So, New Jersey gardeners started working to develop a cabbage that suited New Jersey soil and climate. The Early Jersey Wakefield cabbage was born. Seeds became available to gardeners in the 1860s. It has smooth green leaves and is another conical cabbage. Matures in 60 to 75 days and weighs between 2 and 3 pounds. This is considered a short-season cabbage.

Filderkraut cabbage is an heirloom that comes to us from the Stuttgart region of Germany. It is huge. Its shape is conical, resembling a dunce or gnome hat, and can reach a height of 2 feet with a foot-wide base at the hips. Give this cabbage plenty of room. It has been around since the 1700s, and leaves are sweeter than other varieties. Days to maturity are 100 to 120, so… plant in spring for an autumn harvest. It is listed on Germany's Slow Food Ark of Taste.

Brussels Sprouts

Brussels sprout is the youngest of all varieties of cabbage, and I include it here because… well, it looks like a standard cabbage only in miniature form. It is a food that is either loved or hated. Moms made us eat them after they were cooked to mush and stunk. This stinky odor is due to sulforaphane, which has a sulfur smell.

To make matters worse, they are not easy to grow. They are spoiled brats in the garden.

Sprouts are heavy feeders and need soil that stays moist. A stalk will develop with tiny sprouts or nubs along the stem. If a plant does not get enough nutrients, then the sprouts will not enlarge, which is a huge source of irritation when you have already spent so much time getting them to this point. So, I fertilize with composted manure when seedlings are planted, and then I fertilize again when I see sprouts beginning to form. Sometimes, I even give it a feeding of liquid inorganic fertilizer just to make sure.

This plant was present around 1785. However, evidence of its earlier existence is inconclusive.

They were cultivated around Brussels, Belgium, and thus named for the city. The 'sprout' denotes the part which we eat that grows from the main stem. Sprouts are actually immature buds that grow at the axial or junction of a leaf stem and stock. The top of the central stem never develops into anything other than leaves. These leaves are also edible and can be used the same as cabbage leaves. The presence of Brussels sprouts was recorded in England and France around the 18th century. They arrived in North America in the 19th century.

A vertical growth pattern allows for interplanting among lettuce, carrots, or beets in spring. These plants will be in your garden most of the gardening season, from spring to early winter. They are biennial but grown as annuals. Germinating seeds will follow the same guidelines as cabbage seeds. I start seeds indoors in March and transplant them into the garden when they have two true leaves. At this point, a late hard frost might kill them, so I cover them with an empty gallon plastic jug. The jug, such as a milk or vinegar container, has had the bottom cut out and no cap. It acts as a small greenhouse.

Full sun is required, along with adequate and continuous moisture about 1 inch per week. A frost in fall adds sweetness to sprouts, and harvesting is from the bottom of the stalk up. When sprouts are beginning to develop, I pull the leaf and leaf stem off, which is located just below the sprout. This allows nutrients to go to the sprout instead of the leaf. Don't leave sprouts on the stock too long because they will burst open, and then they are useless.

Long Island Improved is an heirloom from the 1890s from Long Island, New York. This one was the most important commercially grown sprout before hybrids were developed. Green sprouts are on a short 2-foot stalk and need 100 or more days to mature. Harvest when sprouts are 1 ½ inches in diameter. It is a workhorse producing 50 or more sprouts on one stock over a growing season.

Red Rubine is a red/purple Brussels sprout. An heirloom, it needs 90 days to reach maturity. So, planting in mid-summer for a late fall harvest is optimum. Stocks can reach 3 feet tall, and the whole plant is a gorgeous purple-red. A good splash of color to the garden. It is frost tolerant, and frost sweetens the sprouts. Purple sprouts originated in the 1940s by crossing a purple cabbage with a green Brussels sprout.

Groninger is a green landrace sprout. Which means what? The term landrace designates an animal or plant that has developed and changed genetically without any artificial interference. It has adapted to its natural environment without the aid of modern science. These sprouts need 90 to 100 days to mature and are harvested when sprouts reach 1 inch in diameter. So they are on the small to medium size for sprouts.

Roodnerf is an open-pollinated sprout originating from Hurst, England. Plants will reach up to 3 feet tall, and sprouts are 1 ½ to 2 inches in diameter. It is ready to harvest in 100 days.

What is the difference between heirloom, open-pollinated and hybrid? A plant that has been around for at least 50 years is considered an heirloom. Heirlooms are open-pollinated plants that need a pollinator to produce seeds. Pollinators could be insects, birds, wind, or even humans.

Seeds from open-pollinated plants will produce the same as the parent plants. Packets of open-pollinated seeds have a symbol of OP. If you are saving seeds, then open-pollinated seeds are the ones to save.

Hybrids are intentionally developed by crossing two different varieties of a plant to capture the best traits of both. Breeders take two varieties, and usually hand pollinate to develop the desired results. This process can take years of growing, pollinating, and then testing. Growing hybrids in your garden will still need the standard pollinators, i.e., insects, birds, or wind, to develop that hybrid cabbage, but the resulting seeds from that cabbage will not produce true to its parent plant. Packets of hybrid seeds have a symbol of F1. The symbol F1 means 'filial 1,' which is the first child or offspring.

What does all this mean to the home gardener? One is not better than the other. If you have a favorite, then grow it. But, by planting heirlooms, you are then keeping a variety alive with the diversity of information in its genetic pool that has been around for ages.

Chapter 5: Chameleon Cabbages

There are so many chameleon cabbages. Broccoli and cauliflower are two of them. Which means what? It means that broccoli and cauliflower are the same genus and species as cabbage but look totally different. They are different cultivars born from mutations in nature and then manipulated by a curious ancient farmer. Broccoli has a flowering head, which we eat, and cauliflower has a non-flowering head, which we eat. Both have been cultivated for 2000 years. Along with all other cabbages, broccoli, and cauliflower are in the Brassicaceae or cabbage family.

The Etruscans of southern Italy or Sicily are credited with cultivating broccoli. Romans and Greeks dined on it. Romans introduced broccoli to Northern Europe. It was mentioned in France in the mid-1500s. In England, it was a strange plant with the name of

'Italian asparagus' in the 1700s. So, next time you find yourself casually thumbing through a medieval cookbook, you will notice an absence of broccoli in recipes. Leaf and hard-headed cabbages, onions, and garlic were known and eaten in medieval times and probably cooked beyond recognition, but broccoli is absent.

Here, in this country, Thomas Jefferson experimented with broccoli in his garden, but it was still considered an exotic plant. Acceptance and reintroduction in the US came with the immigration of two Italian brothers to California in the early 1900s. Growing and sending broccoli back to Italians on the East Coast, a family business was born. Finally, the American public caught on to broccoli in the 1920s. The company that they established is Andy Boy. California produces around 90% of US broccoli today, which is still harvested by hand.

Broccoli is a biennial plant, which means it completes its growing cycle over a two-year period. But it is grown as an annual. There are three varieties of broccoli. Heading, sprouting, and Romanesco. If not harvested or if plants bolt due to excessive heat, then the flower buds mature and open. Left growing into its second year, broccoli will flower again, and this gives bees some much-needed early spring nectar.

The first variety is heading broccoli, which is the standard large green head that comprises hundreds of immature flower buds and stems.

The most common heading variety is **Calabrese**. It is an heirloom developed in the Calabria region of Italy and was brought to North America by Italian immigrants in the 1880s. It matures between 60 to 90 days and can reach a height of 3 feet. The dark green heads can grow up to 8 inches across. Side shoots of smaller broccoli heads will develop after harvesting the main head if the plant is left to grow.

DeCicco is another Italian heirloom variety. Maturing between 60 to 70 days, it produces a head that is smaller, reaching 4 inches across. The color is blue-green. It will also produce side shoots. Plant height can reach 2 to 3 feet.

Belstar variety is a hybrid that produces medium green heads. It is more heat tolerant than the heirlooms and produces heads that are around 6 inches across. It matures in 60 days and is resistant to downy mildew and heat stress. The plant reaches a height of 2 feet. It is a good choice for Southern states. A hybrid is deliberately crossing two different varieties to produce a third. Seeds from a hybrid will not germinate true to the parent plant, but bees still love the flowers.

The second variety is sprouting broccoli. It does not form an initial large central head but produces multiple small heads on thin stocks. It has a long growing season. In my region, planting in fall, will keep it producing through winter into early summer. It tolerates cold weather, surviving temperatures to 10F. Pinching the apical or main shoot will encourage the development of side shoots.

Early Purple Sprouting broccoli is an heirloom from England. Plants reach 2 to 3 feet in height and are hardy to 10 F. It will develop lots of small side purple heads.

Romanesco broccoli is the third variety and is somewhere between broccoli and cauliflower. It is chartreuse in color, growing in a fractal form, and has been around since the 16th century in Italy. A fractal is a mathematical growth pattern that develops uniform spirals. It is alien-looking. It will catch young gardeners' attention.

Germinating broccoli seeds will follow the same guidelines as germinating cabbage seeds. Days to germination, as with any cabbage, is short, between 5 and 15 days. Tiny poppy-sized seeds will develop into 3-foot plants. They need full sun, soil temperature between 55F and 75F, and seed depth ¼ inch. I start my plants indoors in small pots, laying a few seeds on the surface of moist soil, then adding a small portion of soil to cover. Seeds are so tiny they fall into soil crevices. Gently pat the soil down. In early spring, after two true leaves develop, I put them outside under floating row covers to harden off. Hardening off is acclimating plants to outside temperatures with limited protection.

Developing plants need consistent moisture from germination to harvesting. Broccoli are heavy feeders. They are happy with lots of composted manure. Most broccoli do not tolerate heat well. Air temperature between 55F and 75F is optimum. Plants will bolt in the summer heat. What is bolting? A plant bolts due to excessive heat. It has a growth spurt that develops flowers and seeds before being ready for harvest. In the case of broccoli, the tiny flower buds that you eat will open. At this point, your broccoli needs to be trimmed in order to produce side shoots, hopefully when the weather cools down. Seeds remain viable for 5 years if kept in a cool, dark area.

Broccoli contributes vitamins C, K, iron, fiber, and potassium, along with a host of other essential minerals to the diet. As with any vegetable, eating it raw, you reap the most benefit. When you are munching on broccoli, you are actually eating a cluster of immature flower buds.

The word 'broccoli' is an Italian plural form of broccolo, which translates to flowering crest.

Its root word is from the Latin 'brachium' for branch or arm.

Two common pests for broccoli are aphids and cabbage worms.

Aphids are tiny soft-bodied insects that suck sap from plants, mainly leaves. While this action may not kill your plant, the punctures in the plant tissue might become an area for diseases to take hold. The sap is sugar, and this can attract ants. So, if you have a multitude of ants traveling up and down a plant, the problem may not be ants. It is aphids. Look on the underside of leaves; this is a favorite spot for aphids. Spraying with a water jet or insecticidal soap usually helps control them. If I catch them early, then I just smash or rub them between two fingers. Aphids, along with all other insects, develop resistance to pesticides.

Cabbage worms. Oy vey. They are the bane of every gardener. In early spring, if you notice a small white moth flying around your garden, this is an adult cabbage worm. They are not looking for nectar but looking to lay eggs on the underside of a leaf. These eggs are tiny and hard to see. When it hatches, the larva or worm eats its way to worm adulthood. They are a vibrant, velvety green chewing machine that makes holes in leaves. If left untreated, you will end up with nothing but leaf stems and veins. Then, they transform into pupa and attach themselves to the underside of leaves, stems, or anything else they can find. They spin silk strands for attaching. Putting a row cover over broccoli will keep the white moth from laying eggs. If you find a green worm on a plant or the pupa, which could be a range of colors from yellow to brown and looks like it could be a hibernating worm, just destroy it. Using a broad-spectrum pesticide not only kills the cabbage worm but also all other beneficial insects that you want. The best line of defense is manual labor.

The cabbage family Grand Dame is cauliflower. It is referenced in first and second AD in Europe, but from descriptions, it is hard to determine whether it is broccoli or cauliflower or something in between. The cauliflower that we recognize today is thought to have originated in Cyprus and could be found in Italy in the 12th and 13th centuries. It was introduced to Europe in the 1600s. Louis XIV dined on it, and it could be found growing in Elizabethan English gardens. Its domestication is recent compared to others in the cabbage family. North American seed companies started offering cauliflower seeds in the 1860s.

The head of a cauliflower is not a flowering head. That is a misstatement that appears all too often. It is an inflorescence meristem. Which is what? Meristem is an area located at the tip of shoots or tips of roots and other areas of a plant. It is a group of cells that divide and become specific parts of a plant, such as flower buds, leaves, roots, stems, etc. In the case of cauliflower, the meristem divides but does not differentiate but just keeps continuously replicating itself.

Inflorescence is a cluster of cells that develop in a particular arrangement. With cauliflower, these cells form a spiral that keeps growing outward on the flanks. That is how a cauliflower keeps getting bigger and wider and stays round. So, a cauliflower head will never flower. The edible portion or head of cauliflower is referred to as curd because it resembles cheese curds.

Germinating cauliflower seeds will follow the same as germinating cabbage seeds. As with broccoli, it is a biennial that we treat as an annual. It germinates in 5 to 15 days with full sun. Cauliflower requires room to grow, with up to 2 feet between plants. Broccoli is tall, whereas cauliflower is short and squat. They are heavy feeders, which I fertilize with composted manure twice during the growing season.

Today, cauliflower comes in a range of colors, not just white. Keeping white cauliflower white means shading it from sunlight. Gathering plant leaves, pulling them over the cauliflower head, and then tying them together to form a tent. It can be labor intensive. Some varieties are labeled 'self-blanching' or described as having wrapping leaves. This means plant leaves tend to curl inward and over the cauliflower head, shielding it from sunlight. If exposed to sunlight, a cauliflower will turn yellowish. Still edible but not pure white. They are high maintenance-demanding creatures, but it is always a pleasant surprise to check on a cauliflower, and all of a sudden, there is a small developing white ball at the center. A sense of accomplishment.

Cauliflower attracts the same nuisance pests as broccoli. You might find a cauliflower head that shows signs of loose curds. Curds are not tightly packed and are separated. So, living up to the reputation of a grand dame, conditions that promote loose curds could be wrong soil conditions, weed competition, over or under-watering, not enough fertilizer, temperatures too high or too low, and the list goes on. So, yes, everything needs to be aligned in the universe.

If subjected to adverse heat, inadequate moisture, or lack of nutrients, some cauliflower will exhibit a slight pink blush on the undersides. It is just reacting to environmental stress and is still edible. Seed viability is 5 years if kept in a cool, dark area.

Vitamins C, K, and B6 are in generous supply, along with an assortment of minerals. Folate is present, which is another B vitamin, and is needed to make red and white blood cells.

Our word cauliflower is derived from Italian cavolfiore which translates to flowering cabbage. It derives from the Latin 'caulis,' meaning stem, and 'flor,' meaning flower. So cauliflower has been given a name that has stuck to the premise that a part of the plant that we eat are flower buds. They are not. You are eating a group of cells that are delicious.

Rober cauliflower comes to us from Poland and is somewhat heat tolerant. It is white, and the head can reach 12 inches across.

Snow Crown is a white hybrid and matures in 50 to 60 days. Heads can reach 7 to 8 inches across, weighing 1 to 2 pounds. This is an All-American Selection winner. AAS tests and evaluates new varieties for home gardeners. This variety has been rated as one of the easiest to grow.

The Purple of Sicily is, as you might suspect, purple. An Italian heirloom that, when cooked, changes from purple to green. It matures in 90 days, is insect-resistant, and has a sweet taste.

Amazing cauliflower is appropriately named. It is easy to grow and matures in 75 days. It comes with self-blanching leaves that protect the head from sun, heat, and cold. It retains flavor and quality in the garden, so if you have planted more than one, you don't need to harvest all at the same time. It would be nice if all vegetables had the ability to retain their peak readiness until you decide to harvest. Nature doesn't work that way, but this cauliflower does its best.

Chapter 6: Chilis Or Peppers?

Of all plants that originated in the Americas, it is chili that has the most impact on food. Today, it is hard to find a cuisine anywhere that does not incorporate either sweet or hot chilis into national dishes. Only far northern people such as Laplanders, Mongols, and Eskimos have not incorporated them into their respective cuisines. Before Columbus' trip in 1492, there were no chilis outside of the Americas. Think about that for a moment. All cuisines that have evolved with chilis in their dishes did not exist, nor do you find words in their respective languages for chilis.

After years of petitioning and some respectable begging for financing, Queen Isabella of Spain finally backed Columbus. Her husband, King Ferdinand, was not totally on board with the endeavor. Columbus set sail, landing on the island of Haiti and the Dominican

Republic known as Hispaniola. He didn't know where in the world he was... literally. He was looking for a shorter route to the Indies, which encompassed India, Southeast Asia, and the Malay Archipelago. He was searching for spices, particularly black pepper, known in Spain as pimienta. The word 'indies' refers to the Indus River. This large area was under the cultural influence of India until Dutch, Spanish, and Portuguese trading vessels found their way east, searching for spices. At that point, it was known as the East Indies.

Landing in Hispaniola, Columbus found an unfamiliar spicy hot fruit instead of black pepper.

Ignoring the native term for the plant, which was chili, he gave it the masculine name 'pimiento.' Black pepper was feminine 'pimienta.' Chilis were deemed stronger and better than black pepper. We have Columbus to thank for the confusion of two names, peppers and chili, given to the same plant. And some gender bias thrown in for good measure.

Columbus found chilis incorporated into the island's cuisine. Hot chili was known as 'caribe,' which meant sharp and strong. Native cannibals were known as Caribe, and the islands became known as the Caribbean. Columbus designated islands of the Caribbean 'West Indies' and natives became 'Indians.' He was handing out names right and left. So, there you have it, the East and West Indies on opposite sides of the world. It just depended on whether you sailed east or west from Western Europe.

Chili seeds were dispersed throughout the world primarily thanks to the Portuguese. When Spaniards discovered gold in the New World, their interest shifted to gold and not spices. At this point, they sold their interest in the East Indies to Portugal, eliminating a lot of competition for the spice trade. Portuguese traders carried chili seeds to Africa, India, and Indonesia. This plant, unlike tomatoes and potatoes, was readily accepted everywhere. Only Europe gave it a lukewarm reception, as Europeans were accustomed to milder flavors. However, the peoples of Africa, Arabia, and Asia welcomed it with open arms.

How did the Portuguese end up dispersing chilis when it was Spain that discovered them? When Columbus returned from his first trip, he landed in Lisbon, Portugal, due to a storm that blew his ship off course. He visited King John ll of Portugal to report on his findings. Queen Isabella of Spain got wind of this meeting. This started a ruckus between the two monarchs over who owned what and where, with absolutely no regard for native populations.

These two Catholic monarchs decided to divide the world in two. An imaginary line of demarcation from pole to pole 370 leagues west of the Cape Verde islands was drawn. A league was a measurement and is equal to about 3 miles. It was officially sanctioned by Pope Alexander VI. Spain acquired virtually the entire Pacific, including all of the Americas, except for the eastern part of Brazil, which is the bulge that sticks out in the Atlantic. Portugal acquired the Brazilian bulge, Africa, India, and Asia. An interesting consequence is that most of South and Central America is Spanish-speaking, while Brazil speaks Portuguese. Another consequence of this imaginary line was that the Portuguese disseminated chili seeds to countries east of the Iberian Peninsula.

Trading vessels brought chili seeds to the west coast of Africa. From there, the migration of seeds went to the eastern coast of Africa. Continuing an eastern migration, seeds traveled to India and onto islands of Southeast Asia. Inland provinces of China, mainly

Szechuan and Hunan, may have received seeds due to the Silk Road, which meandered its way through those areas. All areas readily accepted these hot fruits into their cuisines, and it happened quickly within fifty to hundred years.

Chilis arrived throughout Europe after diffusion in other parts of the world. Ottoman Turks are credited with introducing chili along European trading routes in the mid-1500s. Seeds circled back to North America from Europe with Catholic monks. They brought chilis to Saint Augustine, Florida, and Santa Fe, New Mexico, which are the oldest settlements in North America.

Heat in chilis comes from the compound capsaicin. South Americans didn't know what this compound was, but it was effective as a tool of warfare and torture. Today, we have pepper spray. The highest concentration of capsaicin is in the placenta. This is the white interior part of chili that has seeds attached to it. There are different heat compounds present, but capsaicin produces the majority of heat. Dry or stressful growing conditions will increase the amount of capsaicin. So small environmental changes can result in different degrees of heat and make eating them a game of Russian roulette.

Chilis are fruits, and if you eat a chili, and by surprise, it is hotter than you want, then drink milk or eat a portion of yogurt, which will break that heat bond. All mammals have pain receptors in their mouth and throat that react to heat-producing compounds. Capsaicin forms a bond with pain receptors to give that burning sensation. I plant hot chilis in the front flower bed, and deer typically leave them alone. They are nibbled by young deer just once. But don't go to the bank on that advice. Some seasons, there will be that one that keeps coming back. Birds do not have the same pain receptors, so they are excellent distributors of seeds.

The actual flavor of chili is found in the outer wall, or meat. Carotenoid pigments are associated with flavor. They are also responsible for chili's changing color. All chilis will change color as they mature from green to yellow, orange, purple, or brown, finally ending in red.

Chilis are grown as an annual but are perennial shrubs in the tropics and subtropics. It had already been dispersed over a wide area, probably by birds, by the time first humans arrived in South America 7000 years ago. The fruit that we consume is in the Solanaceae family, along with tomatoes and potatoes. The ancestor of cultivated chili is from a central area south of the Amazon forests of Brazil.

I start my chilis indoors in March. Seeds need to be planted ¼ inch deep and take 1 to 3 weeks to germinate, so be patient. Moist, well-drained soil needs to be in the temperature range of 70F for germination. Using planting trays will give you plenty of chili plants or germinate in 2-inch individual pots. Plants are not frost tolerant. In our area, I put chilis in the garden during the first week of June. Until that time, they are growing in a portable greenhouse. Full sun is needed. I add composted manure into the soil before planting and then a second helping of manure mid-way through the season. Seeds remain viable for 4 years.

The word has found its way into European languages such as Italian pepperone, French piment, German pfeffer, and paprika in the Balkans. Arabs have their filfil ahmar, Java has lombok, and the Japanese have togarashi. In Mexico, chili is still chili, but in North America, the name pepper has stuck.

There are literally thousands of varieties of chilis. They are categorized by a Scoville heat index. Bell peppers have a heat index of 0 to 100. Pure capsaicin has a heat index of around 15,000,000.

Padron chili comes to us from northwest Spain and is a standard in tapas bars. It is small, only 2 inches long, usually green, but can change to red. It is a pimento-type cultivar with a taste that is usually mild, but there is a small percentage that is going to be hot. It is a surprise which one you bite into. Days to maturity are 60, and it will keep producing throughout summer. They are fried whole in olive oil until they begin to blister, sprinkled with sea salt, and served. Padron has a heat index that ranges from 500 to 2500.

Poblano chili originated in the Mexican state of Puebla. It is 4 to 6 inches long, heart-shaped, and has a beautiful dark green sheen. Because of its size and thickness of meat, it is a good chili for stuffing. This one is the choice for chili rellenos. Plants can reach 2 feet tall, and days to maturity are around 70 after it is transplanted outdoors. Plant in full sun and harvest all summer. When dried, they are known as ancho chilis and can be ground into chili powder. If left on the plant, chilis will turn a dark red and probably have more heat than when green. Poblano has a heat index of 1000 to 1500.

Numex Suave Orange chili is a habanero type with a fruity flavor but not as much heat as a true habanero. Fruits are 2 ½ inches long, orange, and somewhat wrinkled. Plants can reach 4 feet tall and will produce fruit all summer. It was introduced in 2004 and has a heat index of 335.

You will come across varieties of chilis that have the Numex name. These have been cultivated at New Mexico State University since 1888. Dr. Fabian Garcia improved local chilis by producing a new pod-type chili. It is called the 'New Mexican' type and is a long green chili, which today is called Anaheim. It was taken to Anaheim,

California, and put into production. Since this first introduction, there have been well over 20 different varieties of Numex chilis. Heat index varies due to the different varieties. Some are mild, and some are hot.

While we are talking about New Mexico, there is also **Hatch** chili. The name indicates that it was grown in Hatch Valley, New Mexico, and is a long green type chili of different varieties. So there is actually no chili that has the name of Hatch. But to be called a Hatch chili, it must be grown in the Hatch Valley. It is a colorful sight to drive through Hatch, New Mexico, and see all the chilis drying on rooftops and strings of bright red chilis hanging in shops.

One variety of chili that does carry the pepper term is bell pepper, with extensive varieties. I have included a number of varieties, such as California Wonder, Canary Belle, Quadrato Asti Giallo, Bull Nose Bell, and King of the North. These are sweet, blocky, and thick meaty chilis. They have a heat index of 0 to 100. They do not produce any capsaicin. The name 'bell' was given due to the shape of the fruit.

California Wonder is the oldest standard green pepper. Heirloom, introduced in 1928, has been in production commercially ever since. Plants reach 2 ½ feet tall and will produce all season. Leaving green bells on the plant, they will eventually turn red. Days to maturity are 75 after transplanting.

Canary bell is a hybrid that produces a bright lemon-yellow pepper. Days to maturity are 100, and plants reach a height of 3 feet.

Quadrato Asti Giallo is an heirloom from Italy that produces big blocky peppers that ripen slowly from green to golden yellow. Days to maturity after transplanting are 70 to 80.

Bull Nose Bell is an heirloom that matures in 55 to 80 days. Bell peppers have lobes at the base of fruit, usually either 3 or 4. This variety is not as elongated as traditional bells, and its lobes have been described as similar to a bull's nose. I have to say I have never been that close to a bull to verify. Thomas Jefferson championed this pepper, and it was a standard in his garden.

King of the North is a red bell and, as the name implies, does well in northern gardens with short growing seasons. A New York heirloom was introduced in 1934. Days to maturity are 60.

Buena Mulata chili is a cayenne-type heirloom introduced by William Woys Weaver from seeds he inherited from his grandfather. His grandfather received seeds from Horace Pippin, an African-American folk artist. Plant produces a multitude of stunning chilis that start as deep purple, then change to salmon, and finally red. So, you end up with a whole range of different colors and shades on the plant. It grows to 2 feet, and chilies are 2 to 4 inches long, curved, and have the diameter of a pencil. Days to maturity are 65 to 70, and the heat index is 30,000 to 50,000.

Sheepnose Pimento chili is an heirloom that is 3 to 4 inches in diameter with thick, sweet, meaty walls. It comes to us from Ohio and has been around since the 1940s. Starts out green, but when it is mature, it is a beautiful bright red. Days to maturity are 70 to 80 after transplanting. The plant will top out at 2 feet tall. It is listed on the Slow Food Ark of Taste and has a heat index of 0. It is a tomato-type cultivar chili because of its similar appearance to a round tomato. Tomato cultivar types are grown in Morocco and Spain, producing high-quality paprika, which is ground-dried sweet chili. It is thought that bell peppers may have developed from tomato-type cultivars.

Lipstick chili is a 4-inch long tapered sweet red chili. It is a pimento cultivar, which might be confusing given the name of the previous chili listed. Sheepnose Pimento is the name of a chili, while Lipstick is actually an example of a different cultivar. Days to maturity are 70, and this chili does well in northern gardens. Plant reaches 3 feet tall and will produce chilis all season. Heat index of 0 to 500. Rumor has it that it was so named due to the similar color of cosmetic lipstick.

Jalapeno chili is probably the most recognizable chili anywhere. Its place of origin is Xalapa, Mexico, with a heat index of 2500 to 8000. Chilis grow 3 to 4 inches in length and 1 inch wide.

They are short and fat. Days to maturity are 65 but continue to produce all season if picked regularly. Chipotles are jalapenos that have been smoked to dry them.

Hot chilis are preserved by drying or pickling. World cuisines have developed signature condiments from chilis. North African Arab countries have harissa, which is a chili paste. The place of origin is thought to be Tunisia. Its main ingredients are chilis, olive oil, and salt.

India has curry powder with its primary ingredient, dried ground chilis. Turmeric and coriander are added, along with a host of other spices and seeds. There are as many varieties of curry powder as there are days in the year with corresponding different amounts of heat.

Korea has kimchi, which consists of fermented cabbage with garlic, ginger, and hot chilis.

Sriracha is a chili sauce of Thai origin. It consists of chilis, vinegar, garlic, salt and sugar. It gets its name from the coastal city of

Si Racha in Thailand. Today, production has been taken over by David Tran, a Vietnamese refugee who settled in California, and his business keeps growing.

Jamaica has jerk spice, which consists of a rather large collection of different spices plus cayenne chili and dried pepper flakes.

American chili powder was invented or concocted around 1892 by a German living in New Braunfels, Texas. It is usually made up of several different ground dried chilis combined with a host of different spices depending on taste preference.

Red pepper flakes are simply ground, dried whole chilis, including seeds.

Mexico has given us salsas, moles, and enchilada sauces, to name a few, plus a host of different bottled sauces such as Tapitio, Valentina, and Cholula, which all include chilis in their recipes.

Ottoman Turks are credited with disseminating chilis into Eastern Europe through the Balkan peninsula. Slavic people from this region called chilis 'peperke,' which eventually became paprika. Ground powder from dried pods has become a staple of Eastern Europe. It is available in sweet, smokey, and hot varieties today and is a mixture of several chilis.

Then there is Tabasco sauce. Tabasco is a chili cultivar, a state in Mexico, and, for the last 150 years, an international hot pepper sauce from Louisiana. This chili is small, about 1 ½ inches long, on a bushy plant, and eating one of these is best described as eating something incendiary. It has a heat index of 30,000 to 50,000. The state of Tabasco is in southern Mexico, bordering Guatemala and Yucatan. The word tabasco probably originated with Cortez in the early 1500s, demanding from local Nuhautl natives the name of their area. Tapachco morphed into tabasco. During the war with Mexico (1846 to 1847), US Marines returned from Mexico to the port of New Orleans, bringing a small hot chili. Seeds from these chilis eventually fell into the hands of the McIlhenny family. They had a plantation located on Avery Island. Edmund McIlhenny grew his first commercial crop in 1868. He kept experimenting with these chilis until he found a sauce he liked. The production process is the same today as it was 150 years ago. Chilis are hand-picked when ripe, and ripeness is determined by a 'petite baton rouge.' Chilis have to be a certain red and are measured against a baton rouge. Then, they are ground into a mash, placed in oak barrels, and aged for three years. It is then strained and bottled with vinegar. He patented his sauce in 1870. It stands a good chance of sitting on every restaurant table worldwide.

Chapter 7: Everyone's Favorite

Of all vegetables, there is at least one that is a constant in every garden. Tomatoes. We are addicted to them.

Botanically, it is a fruit even though you find it in vegetable sections of food stores. The wild ancestor is a weedy vine that grows in northwestern South America. It is still there, and the tomatoes resemble a cherry tomato in size and aren't particularly tasteful.

Indigenous South Americans didn't eat them, and seeds slowly migrated north into Mexico, which is believed to be the center of domestication. Incas didn't eat them, but the Aztecs did.

Migration from South America to Mesoamerica took different avenues. Wind, water, birds, and humans were vehicles for a slow stepping stone trip north. Archaeological and linguistic sources give evidence that the indigenous population of Mexico has the longest historical use of tomatoes.

By the time Spaniards reached Mexico, tomatoes were found in the local markets in different shapes, ranging in colors from yellow to red, and used extensively. It is one of few vegetables, along with onions and garlic, that are cooked, forming the basis of so many different cuisines around the world.

Conquistadors in the 1500s noted that Aztecs made a stew of tomatoes, peppers, wild onions, salt, and protein from the legs and arms of sacrificial victims. Protein has been dropped from the ingredient list, and today, we just enjoy salsa.

Tomatoes reached Europe when Spanish explorers returned home. Spaniards took seeds back along with gold and silver. Little did they know the impact that these seeds would make. Some were intentionally brought back to Europe because a few explorers had grown accustomed to eating them, but most were brought back simply as a curiosity. Europeans regarded tomatoes with suspicion and even some fear. Tomatoes belong to the Solanaceae or nightshade family of plants, and this plant family was already known to Europeans for their poisons, consequently the suspicion and fear.

Seeds arrived in Spain and later wound their way to Italy. The Kingdom of Naples, which encompassed the southern half of the

Italian peninsula, Sicily and Sardinia, was under the control of King Ferdinand of Spain. It was this region from which tomatoes spread throughout Italy.

The first reference places tomatoes in Italy around 1544, becoming a botanical hot item. Aristocrats in Italy wanted plants from the New World for novelty. It indicated their wealth and prestige.

Tomatoes were observed and experienced as an ornamental. A few adventuresome Italians did eat them. However, it took an additional 300 years before mainstream Italians caught on.

Nowhere else have tomatoes become so deeply identified with a nation's cuisine.

France saw its first tomato around 1570 in Provence. From there, it traveled north to Paris.

Tomatoes appeared in England around 1597. Everywhere, there was the same suspicion and fear. It was a combination of the wariness of new foods, current medical theories, and a feeling of superior culinary patterns over inferior American ones.

Tomatoes circled back to the Americas, arriving in North America from Europe. Possibly landing in what today is Florida with Spanish explorers. They are mentioned in the late 1600s in southern parts of North America. Southerners grew and ate tomatoes in a number of different forms. Thomas Jefferson's garden hosted tomatoes. He served them in 1806, urging guests to try one. Most North Americans had the same hesitancy as Europe when it came to consuming tomatoes.

The earliest recipes can be found in 'The Virginia Housewife' cookbook published in 1824 by Mary Randolph. There is only one entry for stewed tomatoes, which involves removing the tomato skin, then adding salt, pepper, and butter and stewing them. Not the most inspiring recipe.

The plants are perennial but are grown as an annual. There are different ways to determine types of tomatoes. Growth patterns, shapes, colors, and days to maturity give us over 7500 choices.

Determinate or indeterminate are two growth patterns for tomatoes. A determinate tomato grows upright, has a bushy appearance, produces flowers, and then fruit ripens all at once. You should not prune a determinate because it will not produce additional flowers. An indeterminate tomato has a vine-like growth, producing flowers all season, with fruit ripening throughout the growing season. An easy way to remember the difference is that determinate tomatoes are determined to grow upright, producing flowers all at once, and indeterminate tomatoes really can't make up their mind which way to grow and will produce flowers all season. It is a bit silly, but it works. The wild ancestor tomato is indeterminate. Which is best? Neither has favorable qualities over the other, but both should be staked for support.

Plum, slicing, and cherry tomatoes are three standard shapes. Plum tomatoes are firm and egg-shaped. They have fewer seeds, less water, and more meat than slicing tomatoes, which is why they are a good choice for sauces.

The most famous plum is the **San Marzano** tomato. It has been grown around San Marzano sul Sarno near Naples since the 1770s. It has been modified over centuries through a series of selections from farmers. San Marzanos have a long plum shape, thin skin, and a pointed tip at the bottom.

A true can of San Marzanos will have a DOP certificate on the can, which signifies tomatoes are from the San Marzano region. Plants are grown vertically in rows; tomatoes are not allowed to touch the ground. Harvesting takes place in August or September; they must be ripe and are picked by hand, usually in the evening. Italians do have their priorities. These tomatoes are always canned whole, never crushed or diced. It is the climate and rich volcanic soil that give San Marzano its distinctive flavor, which cannot be reproduced anywhere else in the world. San Marzanos can be grown elsewhere, but the flavor will not be the same. This tomato is an heirloom and has an indeterminate growth pattern.

The **Roma** tomato is the most common plum tomato found in supermarkets around the world. This tomato is shorter and fatter than San Marzanos. The Roma was developed in Maryland in the 1950s for its fusarium wilt-resistant quality. What is fusarium wilt? Fusarium oxysporum is a soil-inhabiting fungus that enters the plant through the roots. Plants wilt, leaves turn yellow, and the plant eventually dies. It thrives in warm soil with temperatures of 75F or higher.

Romas are a cross between San Marzano, Pan American, and Red Top tomatoes. The advantages are that the fruit is bigger than San Marzano and more productive. It is not considered an heirloom, has a determinate growth pattern, and adapts well to a wide range of soils and climates. Most Roma tomatoes in North America come to us from Mexico, with California and Florida contributing.

Slicing tomatoes are round, globe-shaped, and can weigh a pound or more. Beefsteak is the umbrella name that slicing tomatoes fall under. There are hundreds of heirloom and hybrid varieties.

Mortgage Lifter is an heirloom, has an indeterminate growth pattern, and was developed in West Virginia by Mr. M.C. Byles. He kept crossing different varieties until he found the best, sold the seeds, and paid off his mortgage in the 1940s. He named this tomato in honor of a paid mortgage.

Cherokee Purple is a purple heirloom with an indeterminate growth pattern. Grown by the Cherokee tribe in the late 1890s, this tomato and its history had remained out of sight for almost 100 years. It surfaced, traveling through several different hands. Craig LeHoullier, who collected heirloom tomato seeds in the 1990s, received some seeds from John D. Green of Tennessee. Seeds were given to Mr. Green from a neighbor who had received them from Cherokee Native Americans around the turn of the 20th century. Mr. LeHoullier was told that these seeds were a purple tomato with no name. He germinated them, found a tomato with great flavor, and named it Cherokee Purple. Cherokee Purple hit the market in the mid-1990s.

Cherry tomatoes are marble to golf ball size. Most are round, but some are plum-shaped, referred to as grape tomatoes. All grow in clusters. They have a lot of juice and are a great snack.

Mexican Midget is a round, marble-sized, red tomato. It is indeterminate, so a plant will produce throughout summer. You will not need to buy any clam shells of cherry tomatoes with this one in your garden.

Red Pearl is a meaty grape tomato. Indeterminate so it produces throughout summer. They have a good shelf life due to a thicker skin than other cherry tomatoes. Grape tomatoes are a hybrid from Taiwan. Mr. Andrew Chu from Florida imported some seeds from Taiwan and coined the name grape tomato to distinguish it from cherry tomatoes.

Colors of tomatoes are of every hue today. Black, purple, red, pink, orange, yellow, green, and even white. Some have streaks, stripes, and even bicolor.

Days to maturity are the days that a seed needs to germinate and produce fruit. It varies from variety to variety and is probably the most important criterion that you need. If you live in regions that have short summers, high altitudes, or northern states, then you need varieties that have fewer days to maturity. In western Washington, I keep my plant varieties at 75 days to maturity or less. What happens if you pick a tomato that has a 90-day maturity and you live in a short summer region? The seed will germinate, the plant will grow, flower, and probably produce fruit, but the fruit stands a good chance of not ripening. It just doesn't have enough warm days to complete its cycle.

San Marzano needs 78 days to mature. Roma needs 75. Mortgage Lifter needs 80. Cherokee Purple needs 72. Cherry and grape varieties need between 60 and 70 days. Some varieties need 90 or more. How do you determine your area? Check the USDA Hardiness Zone, reach out to the local Master Gardener chapter, or call your soil conservation district.

I start tomatoes indoors sometime in March. Three seeds are planted in 2-inch plastic pots, which contain a potting mix. Moisten the potting mix before seeding. Seeds need to be ¼ inch deep; pots are covered with a piece of kitchen plastic wrap and placed in a warm indoor spot.

Just lay wrap over the pots. This acts as a small greenhouse. I generally don't have to water again. After 7 days or so, seeds will germinate, and I will remove the plastic. If all 3 seeds have germinated, I give them time to grow, and then I pinch two of the weak seedlings because you want only one plant per pot.

Now, the question is how to keep young tomatoes from getting leggy or thin because you cannot put them outside yet. There are several options. The best is to invest in a grow light. The light needs to be just several inches above the top of a plant, and plants will grow correctly.

The second option is positioning plants next to a sunny window, rotating pots several times a day. This is labor intensive, and you will still end up with some legginess. In my region, we are lucky enough to have daytime temperatures high enough to put trays of plants out in a southern exposure. You put them out in the morning and bring them in at night. Low spring nighttime temperatures will kill your tomatoes.

Or you can use a four-tiered, covered small greenhouse. After the true leaves appear, tomatoes can be moved out to one of these greenhouses. A southern exposure receives more sun, warming faster than the other three directions. Tomatoes are in the greenhouse in April; the sun warms the greenhouse, and that heat gets them through nighttime April temperatures. There, they reside until the middle of May to the first of June. In western Washington, we don't put heat-loving vegetables out until Mother's Day at the earliest. Again, these are options for my region. Your planting dates may be earlier or later than mine.

At this stage, my tomatoes are around 6 or 7 inches tall, ready to be planted in the garden or pots. I rotate planting sites for tomatoes every year. Why? Putting the same type of plant in the same spot year after year eventually depletes the soil of nutrients that a particular plant needs. Also, diseases or pests will find an inviting environment and attack your plant if given an opportunity.

They are planted in moist soil, with the bottom half of the main stem buried. Additional roots will develop from cells on the central stem, further anchoring your tomato. During late May and early June, the air temperature in my area can still be on the cool side for tomatoes. The optimum nighttime air temperature needs to be 60F or above for tomatoes to set fruit. So I watch weather forecasts but usually end up covering individual plants with a plastic jug for additional protection. I use a plastic milk or vinegar jug that has had the bottom cut off and no cap. It acts as a greenhouse, raising air and soil temperature. They stay on until the tomatoes have grown and actually fill the jug.

For those tomatoes that got away from you with leggy, long, thin stalks, you can still plant them. Trim all lower leaves and branches, leaving just the upper 3 or 4 inches of stem with leaves. Lay the tomato down so the stem is horizontal to the soil surface. Dig a shallow trench, gently putting the stem and roots in the trench. Leave just the top 3 or 4 inches of the tomato above ground.

The buried stem section will develop roots if given the chance, so all is not lost.

During peak growing season, tomatoes need about an inch of water per week. When is tomato peak growing season? It is from a blossom set through fruit enlargement. I water the soil around my tomatoes, not the whole plant. My objective is to keep plants as dry as possible, which cuts down risks for fungal development. How do you know if your plant needs water? Stick your finger in the soil around the plant. If the soil is moist, then it does not need additional water. Wait a few days and test again.

Tomatoes are considered heavy feeders. Plants in this category need to be fertilized a minimum of twice. I work composted manure in the soil at the time of planting. As plants start setting fruit, then I fertilize them again.

Whichever tomato you plant, they all need to be staked and planted in full sun, which means at least 6 hours of direct sunlight and soil that has good drainage. I use square metal tomato cages instead of round cone-shaped cages. Cone cages can fall over from the weight of tomatoes.

Square cages have more balance.

The minimum nighttime temperature is 50 degrees, and the maximum nighttime temperature is 75 degrees. So if nighttime temperatures fall below 50 as it does in our area even in July, or nighttime temperature stays above 75 as it does in the south, then tomatoes put growth on hold. Flowers may drop off, decrease pollen production, and misshapen tomatoes, to name a few other outcomes. And if the daytime temperature exceeds 95 degrees, then tomatoes have the same reaction. Those of you in warmer areas of the country know that your tomatoes are just humming right along until the dog days of summer kick in, then tomatoes all of a sudden just sit and sulk. They pick up again in September when temperatures cool. The plant is waiting out the excessive heat of August.

Tomato seeds remain viable for at least 4 years or more if kept in a cool, dry place.

The health benefits of eating tomatoes are great. They are high in vitamins C, A and a good source of potassium. Tomatoes are also a good source of lycopene, which is a substance that gives red and pink fruits that characteristic color. It is an antioxidant that helps protect your body from certain diseases.

There isn't anything more rewarding than picking a tomato from the garden and eating it then and there!

The word 'tomato' comes from the Spanish 'tomate,' which came from 'tomatl' in the Nahuatl language of Central Mexico.

When it arrived in Italy, it was a golden or yellow color, not red. It was given the name 'pomi d'oro,' which means golden apple. When Europeans encountered a new food, they didn't know what to call it. They were not going to give it the native name. They just called it an apple of some sort. We had 'pomi d'oro' for tomatoes then, and it evolved into pomodoro today.

For those who just want one tomato plant or don't want to germinate seeds, there is your favorite nursery, which brings me to a conundrum of what to do with tomato plants purchased in March or April. Nurseries are stocked with healthy, beautiful tomatoes that have grown in greenhouses under artificial light and heat. Those tomatoes think it is June. It is not. So, if you purchase a tomato plant in March, in some regions, you will need to babysit it for several months. Take it outside every morning, placing it up against the south side of your house. This area gets the most sun and will be the warmest. Then you need to bring it in every night. Tomatoes will not survive a late frost and will not grow until the nighttime temperatures stay above 50 degrees.

Will purchasing a nursery tomato give you a head start harvesting tomatoes? Some years, yes, and some years, no. It all depends on your weather. But for those who just want one tomato plant or are not interested in germinating seeds, it is an option.

That brings me to just one more temperature, which is critical: soil temperature. It needs to be above 50F for roots to grow. So, you are waiting for a stretch of spring weather that will start warming the soil. It is amazing how you start paying attention to weather reports other than just keeping tabs on the next storm that is going to blow through.

Some common problems that cause plant or fruit damage are Fusarium wilt, blossom end rot, and cat faecing.

Fusarium wilt is a soil-borne fungus that causes plants to turn yellow and then wilt. It can be brought on by wet soil or soils that are 75F or higher. Fungus enters plants through the roots, causing plants to die. This fungus can stay in soils for years. Plants should be removed, destroyed, and don't plant tomatoes in the same area. Needless to say, it does make life difficult. The best way to avoid the whole issue is to purchase seeds or plants that have been labeled 'VF' attached to their name. The 'V' stands for Verticillium wilt, and the 'F' stands for Fusarium wilt. These varieties have been bred to be resistant to both.

Blossom end rot (BER) is caused by environmental conditions. It is a dark spot that appears on the underside of a developing tomato. Conditions that promote BER can be a dry period during the days when plants are vigorously growing. Cold, wet soil can also be a culprit. The best way to try to avoid BER is to mulch around tomato plants. This will conserve moisture during dry periods and also help keep soil temperature adequate for tomatoes.

Cat facing is something that I run into now and again. It is a series of folds and creases with dark areas that develop on the underside of a tomato. Causes usually are cool nighttime temperatures (low 50s) but also cool daytime temperatures (low 60s). Plant tissue develops abnormally in cool temperatures. What to do about air temperature? Again, in cooler regions, you might hold off planting tomatoes until the air is warm enough. Also, plant varieties that are suitable for your region.

The ever-present TOV or 'tomato on the vine' that we all purchase is a greenhouse tomato. It is a beefsteak-type tomato, which means it is round. TOVs were developed in Italy in the 1990s, and the industry caught on with the Netherlands becoming a major production site. North America started producing them in the late 1990s. There are usually four to six tomatoes in a cluster still attached to the stem, bright, happy red color, same size, have all ripened at the same time, and have a longer shelf life than field-grown tomatoes. What is not to like? Our Canadian neighbors were the first to build huge greenhouses to start their industry, followed by the United States and Mexico. We are now seeing TOVs in different shapes, such as cherry tomatoes, as the industry expands. It is wonderful to have a fresh tomato in the dark days of winter.

So it is January, and you are standing at the kitchen counter making a salad for tonight's dinner. In one of your hands is a tomato, and in the other is a cucumber. The tomato, when purchased, had a pinkish hue, but you knew in the dark recesses of memory that, in time, it would turn to an acceptable red. In the same dark recesses of memory, you knew that when you purchased that cucumber, it was ready to eat right then and there. Why? Tomatoes have the ability to ripen off the vine. All fruits produce ethylene gas, which is a hormone that is a ripening or aging agent.

Some fruits such as tomatoes, bananas, apricots, peaches, or any other soft summer fruit produce enough ethylene gas to ripen after they have been picked. These are called climacteric fruits because the critical period of ripening can occur after the fruit has been harvested. Non-climacteric fruits such as berries, watermelons, cucumbers, peppers, citrus, and eggplant do not produce enough ethylene gas to ripen after harvesting. So they need to ripen on the parent plant.

It is mid to late September, and I end up with green tomatoes every year because plants have run out of growing time with temperatures dropping. What to do with green tomatoes? Green tomatoes will ripen sitting on your countertop. But if you want to speed up the ripening process, then put a banana near or on top of your tomatoes. This will cause green tomatoes to ripen faster. Bananas add additional ethylene gas around the tomato.

So, now, what do I do with all those ripe tomatoes? I have a deep, unexplained fear of canning. I visualize the kitchen walls covered in tomatoes and metal and glass shrapnel embedded in me and the dogs. So, I place my ripe, unpeeled tomatoes on a cookie sheet and put them in the freezer. After freezing, they are put in zip-lock bags and placed back in the freezer. We cook with them all winter. To remove the skins, just place them under tap water for 30 seconds or so; the skins peel easily, and the tomato is still frozen to chop. I am not picky about whether to freeze plum tomatoes or round ones. I just don't want to waste any. A second option is to make tomato sauce and freeze it.

Chapter 8: Scary Potatoes

Potatoes are an annual New World crop belonging to the Solanum or nightshade family. This fourth most important crop is surpassed by rice, corn, and wheat in terms of human consumption. Today, it is found in temperate regions from sea level up to 15,000 feet in elevation on all continents. It has the ability to fit into micro-environmental niches all over the world. Its place of origin is the Andes Mountains of South America. There are more than 4500 varieties and over 100 wild species. They come in a range of colors, from standard white to yellow, purple, and red.

Domestication is thought to have taken place between 10,000 and 7,000 years ago in regions of Peru and Bolivia from findings of potato remains in caves and depictions in artwork. Incas took different varieties and grew them in micro niches at different elevations in the

Andes. You would never find rows of alternating green plants and brown earth. They did not practice monoculture. Their plots were uneven and haphazard, but it worked because of the diversity of crops and taking advantage of microenvironments.

Some potatoes grown at higher altitudes have been freeze-dried for thousands of years.

Tubers are frozen at night, warmed in the sun, trampled to remove any residual water, soaked in water for several weeks, and finally sun-dried. This traditional end product called 'chuno' was easy to transport and could be stored for years before being reconstituted in soups and stews.

Spanish explorers took potatoes back to Europe around the mid-1500s. Its history in Europe is a tough road to acceptance. It took more than three centuries for potatoes to be utilized. It was labeled as poisonous, tasteless, a producer of gas in humans, and an aphrodisiac. Spaniards had never come across a vegetable that was propagated from a tuber instead of a seed nor eaten anything that grew underground.

It was also a time when vegetables were attributed to helping or hindering certain parts of the human body. For example, walnuts were thought to be good for brains because of their similar appearance. Beets were thought to be good for blood because of the red color. Due to their growth pattern, tubers on underground stems were thought to cause leprosy. Its reputation was all over the board, and consuming potatoes was viewed with suspicion.

Antoine Parmentier, a French pharmacist who spent time in a Prussian prison, championed potatoes. He ate potatoes while in prison and grew to appreciate their nutrition. After his return to France, he kept petitioning the Paris Faculty of Medicine about the benefits of consuming potatoes. Finally, in 1772, they were declared edible. Up until this time, potatoes were used for hog food. Even Marie Antoinette took up the cause by sashaying around Versailles wearing potato flowers in her hair. It was the political agenda of the day to get any peasant to eat potatoes.

Peter the Great, in Russia, had just as hard a time convincing local peasants they were going to like potatoes and needed to eat them. I think he carried a big stick. Dissemination into Africa and Asia followed along the same resistance to acceptance.

Potatoes arrived in North America with colonists in the 1600s, but even here, it was not one of the top ten favorite vegetables. Thomas Jefferson helped turn it around. While he served as American Minister to France from 1784 to 1789, he sampled many new foods, including a fried potato. He returned home bringing over 100 recipes, including one for French fries.

It has been credited with fueling the industrial revolution. Potatoes were responsible for alleviating starvation but were blamed for famines in Ireland. In potato's early days in Great Britain, it had a hand in religious intolerance. Protestants in northern England declared potatoes fit for pigs and papists. Ireland had a potato named protestant because they boiled the devil out of it. Places that readily accepted potatoes, such as Ireland, did so not because of an adventurous spirit but hunger. It slowly became known as an anti-famine food with yields per acre higher than grains such as wheat.

Today, they are eaten fresh (boiled, baked, or fried). However, the bulk of potatoes grown are used for processed products such as chips, frozen potatoes, fast food, and animal fodder. Industrial products such as glue, plastic, and some vodka are still made from potatoes. McDonald's has expert potato tasters and is very selective in their choices, using only a few varieties for their fries, all of which are russet potatoes. The majority of potatoes grown in the US are from the Columbia Basin region, which encompasses Washington, Oregon, and Idaho states.

A good source of fiber, carbohydrates, protein, and a whopping amount of vitamins B-6 and C. It is no wonder that the Irish could subsist on practically nothing but potatoes. What is the ultimate comfort food? Mashed potatoes, and for good reason. Contained in potatoes are carbohydrates, vitamins B and C, and some protein. Add some milk and butter, which supplies calcium and fats, and you almost have a complete diet.

The first printed recipe is found in 'The Art of Cookery Made Plain and Simple.' The author was Hannah Glasse, and it was published in 1747 in London. Her recipe called for boiling potatoes, then adding milk, salt, and butter and mashing it all together. Good recipes never need to be changed.

In order for potatoes to develop, three conditions need to be present. First is a sunny spot with at least 6 to 8 hours of sun. Next is a good loamy or sandy soil. Soil needs to be loose and free of good size rocks. Third is adequate water. Watering is needed throughout summer but is crucial when potatoes start to flower and after the flowering stage. The onset of flowers signals that potato tubers are growing.

They are grouped into early, mid, and late-season varieties for maturing. Early potatoes mature within 60 to 80 days. Yukon Gold, Chieftain, and Satina are early varieties. Mid-season potatoes mature within 80 to 100 days. Kennebec and Yellow Finn are mid-varieties. Late-season potatoes mature 100 days and more. Ozette, Russet Burbank, and German Butterball are late varieties.

I plant potatoes in April. If planted too early, a late frost may kill potato shoots. There are two methods of growing potatoes. Sexually, from potato flowers, which will go to seed, or vegetative, from a potato or piece of potato. Those grown from seed will develop tubers but will not be identical to the parent plant. Vegetative reproduction will result in a clone of the parent plant. This method is using seed potatoes.

Seed potatoes are small whole potatoes or pieces of larger potatoes that have several 'eyes' or buds. These can be potatoes from last year's harvest or purchased seed potatoes from garden stores or online nurseries. Make sure to purchase certified disease-free seed potatoes. Do not use potatoes that are sold for consumption. These may have been sprayed with a sprouting inhibitor but also could harbor diseases that you would unknowingly introduce to your soil.

My seed potatoes rest on the kitchen counter until buds begin to develop. Larger potatoes that I have cut into several pieces need three or four days for the cut sides to dry, forming a crust.

This crust helps seal out any potential diseases that might enter, which inhibit it from developing. Potatoes need sunlight and temperature between 60 and 70 F to initiate buds to develop. After the buds begin to swell and grow, they are ready to be planted.

These buds will develop into the whole plant, which includes potato tuber, roots, and above-ground stems and leaves. Potato plants have above and below-ground stems. The underground stem is called a stolon. So… potatoes have both stems and roots growing underground. Tubers that develop on a stolon are storage facilities for the plants that we rob and eat. Leaves produce sugar from photosynthesis, and this sugar is transferred down to the stolen, converted into starch, and tubers develop.

Why are potatoes planted in trenches instead of just digging a hole planting a potato as you do tomatoes? When potato plants start to grow, part of the stem is below the soil surface. Mounding soil around new stem growth increases the length of this underground stem. There are nodes present on underground stems, and it is these nodes that will develop into stolons. Stolens typically grow horizontally and generally do not go much deeper than the depth of a seed potato. The potato tuber develops from a swollen section of a stolon.

The end of a potato growing season is signaled by plants dying back and potatoes being ready to harvest. I normally don't leave mine in the ground due to fall rains in my region. Their skin is thin, so after harvesting, I leave a dusting of soil, which keeps potatoes from losing moisture and becoming soft. This hardening off allows thin potato skins to thicken. Rain or watering at this point could cause potatoes to rot or even try to sprout again.

Wash potatoes when you are ready to cook with them. Store in a relatively cool, dark, above-freezing environment, such as a garage. When you harvest potatoes, you will get different sizes. Even some that are the size of marbles. I call these 'peanut potatoes.' Don't discard them! I put them whole in soups and stews.

Different regions will have slightly different planting times. Check your local extension office, the state university's agricultural departments, or reputable gardening sites.

The size of potatoes depends on the amount of moisture and nutrients available during a growing season. Soil needs to be a sandy or loamy soil, not clay. Typically, potatoes are planted in trenches, but now there are bags that can be used for planting. If planting in a trench, then it needs to be around 6 to 8 inches deep. After the eyes have started to grow, place potato pieces at the bottom of a trench, cut side down and 12 inches apart. Cover with 3 inches of soil and wait. Keep covering with soil as stems and leaves push through the soil. Eventually, trenches are filled, and you are now mounding or hilling soil. So you start with a trench and end with a mound, giving potatoes a good 12 to 15 inches of growing depth.

If using the trench method, I can't stress enough how important it is to rotate where you plant potatoes. Rotation of potato planting every two years cuts down on nutrient depletion but also aids in keeping soil-borne problems from developing.

Another method of planting potatoes is by using a grow bag. They are portable and can be used just about anywhere as long as you have sun. I place straw and soil in the bottom of a bag about 4 inches deep, place seed potatoes on top of the soil, and then cover with another 2 or 3 inches of soil. As seed potatoes develop green stems and leaves, continue to add soil to cover the new growth. This is repeated until the soil has reached the rim of the bag. I lay 6 to 7 seed potatoes in each bag. Along with being portable, another attribute is harvesting in a given amount of space. Some potatoes in trenches are always left simply because you didn't find them. At season's end, empty the soil out, distribute it in the garden, store bags in a dry shelter, and then use new soil next spring. These bags don't last forever, but keeping them dry over winter will give you four or five years of usage. Using grow bags eliminates the need to rotate because I use new soil every year.

If you have grown potatoes, you probably have come across a potato that has started turning green. If this is the case, it has been exposed to sunlight and is developing chlorophyll. Mound soil over exposed potato and problem solved.

Phytophthora infestans is a water mold, and its common name is late blight. It is the scourge of any potato and is responsible for the Irish potato famine. It destroys entire plants and turns underground potatoes into a black mush. It needs a moist, cool environment to develop. Dark splotches first appear on leaf tips or stems. Rain can wash spores into the soil, infecting young tubers. Good news is this fungus survives poorly in native soils and can be killed off by frost. The bad news is infected tubers that are left in the ground create a problem for disease management. It is difficult to control this disease. Host plants for this fungus are in the Solanaceae family, which, along with potatoes, includes tomatoes and eggplant, among others.

Even more scary is the Colorado potato beetle, which isn't from Colorado. It is a pretty yellow oval-shaped beetle with 10 black stripes on its wing covers. The larva is red or orange with a black head and two rolls of black spots down the side of its body. That is about all the positive attributes this insect has. It devastates potato fields. Its original habitat is southern Mexico and was probably brought north, hitching a ride on Spanish explorers' horses and cattle. It vexed farmers for years, and in desperation, a farmer threw some old green paint on his potato plants.

The green color was due to arsenic and copper. It killed the beetle.

So now enter the scientists, and their interest is what else arsenic and copper could control. The birth of the industrial pesticide has begun. It worked for a while, but those beetles just kept adjusting to the pesticides and surviving. Scientists kept coming up with new, more potent concoctions. DDT and others. It is an ongoing battle with farmers pitted against nature's ability to adapt. In the process, we may be poisoning ourselves. In a small home garden, if you have a Colorado Potato beetle, just pick it off and send it to beetle heaven.

Flea beetles are dark-colored chewing insects that are native to North America. Adults chew numerous small holes through potato leaves, and larvae that are underground attack the tuber. If left untreated, flea beetles can help spread other diseases such as wilt and blight. So flea beetles may not cause your potato to die, but a secondary disease such as wilt or blight will kill your potato. I check early in spring when leaves are emerging and spray neem oil. It keeps you vigilant.

There are different types of potatoes. A waxy potato has low starch and high water content, so it tends to keep its shape when cooked. The Yukon Gold potato is a good example of a waxy potato. Floury potatoes have low water content and high starch. Russet potato is a good example of a floury potato. A 'new' potato is any potato that is harvested before reaching a mature size. Today, we have choices of small potatoes of different colors. Fingerling potatoes have a shape similar to our fingers, have a waxy consistency, and come in a range of colors. One of my favorite fingerlings is the Ozette potato.

Ozette is a fingerling type and, of all potatoes that are found around the world today, it did not journey to Europe before winding its way back to North America. Ozettes were brought directly from South America to the Pacific Northwest by Spanish explorers in 1791. In an attempt to colonize western North America, a fort was built at what is now Neah Bay in Washington State. A garden was planted, but after only one year, the fort was abandoned due to severe winter weather. Makah Indians took this potato, incorporated it into their cuisine, and it was rediscovered by the rest of us in the 1980s. It is a member of the Slow Food Ark of Taste and is a late-season variety.

Yukon Gold potato was developed by Canadian Dr. Gary Johnston in the 1960s. It has an eye-free thin skin and butter yellow flesh, so there is no need to peel. The name of Yukon was a tribute to the Yukon River and the gold rush territory of northern Canada. Gold was added because of its yellow flesh. They tend to keep their shape after cooking and are good candidates for boiling or sautéing. It is an early-season potato.

Russet potato is the most familiar in North America and has a long family history line. It started in the 1870s with Luther Burbank. From his truck farm in Massachusetts, he planted some potato seedlings that were developed from an Early Rose seed ball. Because development was from a seed ball and not a clone, there were several varieties growing. One caught his eye, and he took clone cuttings and replanted. It became known as the Burbank potato. He then sold the rights to his potato for $150 and moved to California. He experimented, bred, and introduced over 800 strains and varieties of plants. We have Shasta daisies, Elberta peach, Elephant garlic, plumcot, and Santa Rosa plum, among a long list of others for which to thank him.

Then, a variation of the Burbank with a lighter brown russet-colored skin was developed by Mr. Lou Sweet in 1914. It became known as the Russet Burbank potato. Typically, fast food fries are russet potatoes. It is a late-season potato; the flesh is white and mealy, which makes it an excellent choice for baking or fries. Today, we have bags of 'russets,' also known as 'Idaho potatoes' everywhere.

A potato that I plant every year is **German Butterball**. It was introduced in 1988 by David Ronniger of Idaho. It has a yellow, waxy flesh, russet-colored skin, is generally round in shape, and stores well through winter. It is a late-season potato maturing in 100 days or more and is great fried, mashed, or boiled.

Irish Cobbler has been around since 1876. Origin is not known but is thought to have come from Irish shoemakers in the northeastern US. It is a round potato with white flesh and white skin, an early potato maturing between 60 and 80 days, and makes great mashed potatoes.

Norland is a round red potato developed by North Dakota State University in 1957. An early potato maturing between 60 and 80 days, with white flesh and great for salads and boiling.

When you buy a bag of small red potatoes at your market, there is a good chance that you are buying Norlands.

The beginning of the potato chip was not one of ingenuity but of exasperation. George Crum, a chef working in Saratoga Springs, New York, in the 1850s, happened to serve fried potatoes to a picky diner who sent them back to the kitchen because they were too thick. George fried another batch, which was also rejected. The story continues with an exasperated George slicing potatoes paper thin and frying. It was a hit, and word spread. I can't imagine how anyone could hand-slice enough potatoes for chips to serve in a restaurant. Mechanical slicing machines finally arrived in the 1920s. Up to this point, chips were mainly a New England item. Now, enter Herman Lay in the 1920s in the South. He started out selling his chips from his car to grocers and later founded the Lay Distributing Co.

Tater tots were introduced in the 1950s by two brothers, Nephi and Golden Griggs. They had a farm on the Oregon-Idaho border growing corn and potatoes. The frozen food industry was just getting started, and they wanted in on the action. They started processing and freezing potatoes, but there was waste. They took slivers and pieces of irregular potato and smashed them together into small round globes. Fried until golden brown, they are today a common food snack in schools and fast food. The company Ore-Ida was born.

Our word potato evolved from Spanish patata. There are several slang words for potatoes in the English language. Spud comes from Middle English, referring to a tool used for digging or lifting something out of soil. It was recorded in New Zealand English around 1845, referring to a potato. Mickey is a term for a roasted potato from the Depression era. Murphy is a common Irish name, and potatoes become known as Murphys as a derogatory name. Tater is just a short version of potato.

Chapter 9: Roots and More Roots

Carrot

Botanically, a carrot is a root, or taproot, and a far cry from its spindly ancestor, which was colorless, bitter, and tough. Today, it is a fat, juicy, sweet root that is found in every cuisine. It is in the Apiaceae family or parsley family, along with parsnip and a wide range of herbs. In antiquity, wild carrot seeds and leaves were utilized both as an herb and medicine. In North America, a weed that goes by the name of Queen Anne's Lace is a wild carrot.

It is an Old World plant, and wild plants are still found growing in Europe, North Africa, and Eastern Asia. Seeds have been found in the Switzerland, Germany area dating back 4000 to 5000 years ago. In Greek and Roman classical times, carrots and parsnips were often confused with one another. Both were white, about the same size, and had two names that were used interchangeably. So, the history of carrots and parsnips at this point is a bit murky.

The domesticated carrot has its place of origin in the region of Afghanistan, which was under Persian influence around 900 AD. Through natural mutations, cultivated carrots of this region developed into purple and yellow carrots. Two subspecies developed with purple and red carrots traveling east, probably along the Silk Road, from Afghanistan, reaching India, China, and later Japan in the 14th to 17th century.

The yellow subspecies traveled west into Europe, developing into the orange color we associate with carrots today. Arabs brought carrots to Spain during the Arab expansion in the 12th century. From there, they spread to other areas of Europe. Romans were enjoying purple carrots in the 14th century. Colonists arriving in 17th century North America brought carrots. Carrots were mostly yellow mutants during this period. It was the Netherlands that took carrots into their orange color during the 17th century. From this original orange carrot, all modern varieties were developed.

The word 'carrot' traveled just about as far as the actual carrot. English 'carrot' was mentioned around 1530, which descended from Middle French 'carotte.' This came from the Late Latin 'carota,' which came from the Greek 'karoton,' which came from an Indo–European word 'ker,' which meant horn.

Carrots are a biennial cool weather crop that we grow as an annual. Their life cycle actually covers two growing seasons. We harvest carrots in the first year of this cycle. Photosynthesis occurs, sugar is made in leaves and then it is transported down into roots. The root swells with this sugar and we enjoy sweet, fat, carrot roots. The actual stem on a carrot at this point is tiny. Next time you find yourself face to face with a carrot that still has a green leafy top take a look at the junction between root and leaf stem. You will see a tiny stem that leaves are growing from sitting on top of the shoulder of the root. Really. It is there. If left to continue into a second growing season carrots will flower producing seed. The sugars that have been stored in the root are now transported up into a stem which elongates and flowers will form. Roots now develop fiber or shrivel due to lack of sugars. Carrot flowers have the same configuration as Queen Anne's Lace.

Sow seeds in spring as soon as soil can be worked, but also around the middle of July for a fall crop. Soil needs to be loose, well-drained, but moist. For carrots to grow straight a good sandy or loam soil is required. I use a hand held cultivar to work an area that I am planting.

I want my soil to be of a crumbly consistency and loose about six or seven inches deep. Carrots are considered light feeders so I work composted horse manure into an area before sowing seeds then smoothing the surface.

After seeds have emerged, I place straw alongside each carrot row. The straw keeps weeds at bay but also will eventually become mulch to be worked back into soil. A rocky or hard soil will give you misshapen, forked or stunted carrots. Any obstruction to the root such as rocks will cause it to correct the growth direction, ending with strange looking carrots. Optimum soil temperature for planting is 55F to 75F. Optimum air temperature is 50F to 85F. Sugar levels will be highest in this temperature range. Carrots can withstand a light frost.

Seeds are small enough to be placed directly on the soil surface. Some will fall down into crevices of soil. Then, take additional soil, sprinkling it over the area to a depth of ¼ to ½ inch, patting it down. Carrot seed planting depth ranges from almost the soil surface to about a ¼ inch deep, depending on which variety. Read your seed packet.

If planting multiple rows, rows need to be 16 to 24 inches apart. It takes around 2 to 3 weeks for seeds to germinate and poke their heads up. So don't be discouraged. I try not to plant in long rows, so I have small rows of carrots, maybe three feet long, in several locations. There are always too many seeds germinating in a row so they grow crowded together and need to be thinned. How do you know when a carrot is ready to harvest? I have two ways to determine size. I look at leaf stems. The thickest leaf stem will have the biggest carrot. Also, brushing soil from the shoulders of carrots will show you the carrot diameter. It is not a perfect science, but most of the time, it works.

Carrots do not do well in summer. After temperatures rise above 80 F, carrots can become woody and bitter-tasting. Growing carrots intensively with peas, beans, onions, or leeks is a good combination. Also, planting radishes with carrots is a good combination. Radishes germinate quickly and are harvested, while carrots are just getting started.

Full sun is needed. Carrots also do well in areas that have partial or dappled shade. Days to maturity start around 55, depending on the variety. Harvesting can be at any stage of carrot growth, and thinning is a must to avoid misshapen or stunted carrots. You have to give them room to grow. Carrot seeds remain viable for three years. The US major production area is California, with Texas and Florida contributing also.

So, you are going to harvest some carrots, pulling one up. What a surprise! The carrot looks awful with black/brown holes, tunnels, and even some soft spots, but the green leafy tops look healthy. You, my friend, have carrot rust fly. It is an annoyingly tiny fly that lays eggs on the soil surface in May or June. Eggs hatch, and maggots travel down into the soil along the carrot root. They feed on carrots, leaving black spots. Maggots reach adulthood, changing to a pupa. The pupa remains in the soil and eventually develops into another carrot rust fly. This cycle takes place over a 3 to 4-month period. So, in areas with long warm seasons, there could potentially be several life cycles of this fly. Then they overwinter in the soil, starting over again next spring. To help avoid this critter, plant carrots in late May. This will do away with the first generation of flies. Covering carrots with floating row covers will keep females from laying eggs. The most important is to rotate the planting area for carrots. What do you do with black spotted carrots? I put them all in a plastic bag (with or without spots), close the bag, and throw the bag in the trash. You want to break this life cycle. Then, I plant seeds again in a different location. Any larva left in the ground has been robbed of a food source.

Carrots are high in beta-carotene, vitamin C, and a good amount of potassium. They have a low glycemic index number, which measures how fast bodies convert sugar into blood sugar. They are digested with a slow absorption rate, which is good for you.

The popular bags of baby carrots found in grocery stores started out as full-size carrots that are peeled and chopped down to a consistent 2-inch size. In the 1980s, Mike Yurosek, a California farmer, wanted to stop wasting carrots that had blemishes or were misshapen. These were not perfect enough for food stores ending up as juicing carrots, animal fodder, or just thrown away. So he took his imperfect carrots, cut them down to snack size, packaged them, and it was a hit.

Carrot colors range from white, yellow, orange, red, and purple to black. All carrots have fiber, minerals, and vitamins. White carrots have no pigment, hence their white color, but they have dietary fiber, which can help against colon cancer. White carrots are a good alternative for those who are allergic to carotene. Yellow carrots have some beta-carotene and lutein. Lutein has been linked to eye health, perhaps slowing macular degeneration. Xanthophyll is a compound that gives yellow carrots their color. Orange carrots have the highest amount of beta-carotene, which is the pigment that makes carrots orange. Beta-carotene is an antioxidant that, as the name implies, keeps cells from becoming damaged due to oxidation. The pigment that gives red carrots their color is lycopene, which is also found in red tomatoes, another antioxidant. Purple or black carrots usually are dark on the outside, but slicing one reveals an orange center. This color is due to yet another antioxidant, anthocyanin. What to take away from this range of colors? All carrots are healthy and full of antioxidants, fiber, minerals, and vitamins.

One last color. Green. What to do if some of your carrots are green at the top of the root or shoulder? Top of the root has been exposed to the sun, which causes the exposed area to turn green. Just mound the soil around the carrot to cover the exposed root. The green color will cause a bitter taste.

It might come as a surprise that there are several different types of carrots depending on their root shape and length, not just the standard 8 to 12-inch long orange type. And all of these types of carrots have numerous varieties.

Globe is the smallest type. **Paris Market** or **Parisienne** are two round, short orange varieties. They are 1 to 2 inches in diameter and 2 inches long. They have a short growing season, maturing in just 55 days, and a great one for children to grow. Because this variety is short, it is a good choice for planting in rocky soils or soils that contain high amounts of clay. It is also a good choice for container gardening. These are French heirlooms that have been around since the 1850s. This variety does not store well, so harvest and eat them!

Chantenay is short and stout, growing 5 to 6 inches long. **Caracas** is an orange variety I have grown. It matures around 60 days, is conical in shape, is a good candidate for square-foot gardens, and does well in heavy soils. Caracas fits in the palm of your hand. It is an adorable carrot that you can rinse off and enjoy in the garden. **Red Cored Chantenay** carrot is another heirloom orange with a red-orange core. This variety was introduced in 1929 by C.C. Morse &

Co. It can be harvested in 70 days. It stores well, making it a good carrot for soups and stews.

The **Danvers** variety is a true American heirloom developed for the rocky soils of Danvers, Massachusetts, in the late 1800s. It was marketed by Burpee Seed Company in 1886. It is a medium-sized orange carrot attaining 7 inches in length. It is blocky, almost cylindrical in shape. At the top of the root, it reaches a diameter of around 1½ inches, then tapers slightly to the root end. It does well in typical New England rocky soils. It is ready for harvesting between 65 to 75 days after germination and stores well. **Danvers** and **Danvers Half Long** are two orange varieties. A purple carrot is **Cosmic Purple**. This is a purple-skinned carrot with yellow flesh developed in Madison, Wisconsin, at the USDA ARS in 2005. It is ready to harvest 60 to 70 days after germination.

The **Nantes** carrot is an heirloom from the region of Nantes, France, developed in the 1850s by French botanist Henri Vilmorin. It was introduced to the US in the 1870s. It is orange, typically 7 inches long, but fat. One carrot can weigh a pound. This is another carrot that is almost cylindrical in shape. **Scarlet Nantes** carrot is red-orange, is ready to harvest in 65 to 75 days, and adapts well to different locations. **Touchon**, another heirloom variety from France, is ready to harvest in 65 days, producing 6 to 8-inch orange carrots. It stores well and makes excellent juice.

Imperator carrots are long tapered roots and are the commercial type of carrot. It was developed in 1924 by Associated Seed Growers crossing Nantes with Chantenay carrots. Deep sandy/loam soil is necessary because they are long carrots. **Atomic Red** is one variety. It is ready to harvest 65 to 75 days after germination, growing up to 11 inches long. When harvested, they are a dull pink, but cooking them will turn them scarlet. To plant any Imperator carrot, the soil needs to be loamy or sandy and tilled or worked down to a depth of 12 to 15 inches. These are deep carrots. Obstructions such as rocks need to be removed as they will hinder the growth of long, straight carrots. My soil is glacial till, which means I am lucky enough to have a never-ending supply of rocks of different sizes. So, I never turn my soil that deep. Imperator carrots can be harvested at an early stage before reaching a long length if you have rocky soils.

Beet

Beets, along with Brussels sprouts, okra, liver, and anchovies, are either loved or hated. There is no in-between. The reason for the love-hate relationship of beets is their earthy flavor. Sometimes beets have this taste, and sometimes they do not. It all depends on the levels of a substance called geosmin. The word means 'earth smell,' and it is created by bacteria in soil. It is responsible for that earthy taste in beets, the sweet smell of warm, moist soil, and the 'muddy' taste of some drinking water. It is not harmful for human consumption.

Beets belong to the Amaranthaceae family, along with amaranth, spinach, and a long list of others. The ancestor of the beet is a sea beet, which is an Old World plant that grows along the coasts of the Mediterranean and Middle East, producing edible leaves. Ancient Egyptians, Greeks, and Romans cultivated it for its leaves, not the thin, fibery root.

Romans are credited with cultivating table beets, which have an edible root. It was the Romans that spread beetroots throughout Northern Europe. Beet leaves are also edible, either raw in salads or cooked, similar to spinach.

It is a biennial but grown as an annual. If left for its second year, it will send up a stock that will flower, producing seeds. At this point, the beetroot is fibrous. There are three types of beets: table beets, sugar beets, and mangold beets. Table beet is the beetroot we eat. It is referred to as beets, table beet, red beet, garden beet, and beetroot. Sugar beets were developed in the mid-1700s in Silesia, a region that today is southwestern Poland. The King of Prussia was looking for a source of sugar other than sugarcane. Today, the root is white, contains 20% sugar, and supplies about 60% of the sugar produced in the US. Sugar obtained from sugar beets or sugar cane is the same sugar. Mangold beets are grown for animal fodder. Beets have the highest concentration of sugar in all vegetables.

The word 'beet' comes to us from the Old English 'bete' from the Latin 'beta,' which could be of Celtic origin.

It is a cool weather crop that does best in soil temperatures between 50 to 85 F and air temperatures between 45 to 85 F. Beets don't thrive in warm weather. Soil needs to be loose sandy loam, not heavy or clay. They are heavy feeders, so I fertilize them with composted horse manure before seeding. Seeds are planted directly into the soil as soon as they can be worked in spring. I fertilize again during the growing period.

The seed you plant is actually a seed ball containing several seeds. Seeds take 1 to 2 weeks to germinate, so be patient. After germination, thinning seedlings is required. Some years, I lift the seedlings out, separate them, and replant them. Beet seedlings don't like this, usually sulking for a week or so, then they pick up and get on with their business. Other years, I just cut the tops off some seedlings, which will thin them. Cutting tops off eliminates disturbing the roots of other beets.

Full sun is required, or partial shade if in warmer climates. Evenly watered soil is a must for any location.

Days to harvest range between 45 to 65 days. They should not be larger than 3 inches in diameter. Roots could become woody if left to grow larger. How do you know when a beet is ready to harvest? Some beets will have their shoulders above soil level, and you can see the diameter of the beet. Others may need to have soil brushed from them to determine the diameter. Don't throw the leaves away! Wash and steam them as you would spinach. They are sweeter than spinach and delicious. Seeds remain viable for 4 years.

Leaf spot is a disease that could develop due to overhead watering at the wrong time of day. Watering should be done in the morning to give leaves a chance to dry before nightfall. Also, overcrowding of plants, which reduces air circulation, can cause damage.

Leaf miners are insects that live in the leaf tissue. You end up with squiggly lines on your leaves. So, if you have a leaf that resembles a mountainous road map, then pick damaged leaves off and discard them in the trash.

Beets are a good source of folate, which is a B vitamin, fiber, vitamin C, and manganese.

Crosby's Egyptian beet has been around since late 1800. Josiah Crosby was a market farmer from the Boston area who refined this strain, which had originated in Germany. The beet, as far as anyone can tell, had nothing to do with Egypt except to put an exotic spin on the beet and enhance its marketability. It is not round but has a flat top and bottom. It matures in 60 days and should be around 3 inches in diameter. Some portions of the beetroot may be above the soil line. This is ok.

Crapaudine or **Lady Toad** beet might be the oldest beet, having about 1000 years under its belt. It is French in origin and was introduced to the US in the 1860s. It grows elongated and deep, similar to a carrot. Its skin is black, resembling tree bark with occasional gnarled bumps and rootlets. The skin isn't easy to remove, but the taste is worth the effort.

Golden beet has sweet, gorgeous yellow flesh and is ready to harvest in 55 days. Grow to just 2 inches in diameter in loose soil. This heirloom was introduced by Burpee Seed Co. in the 1940s.

Chioggia beet is an heirloom from Chioggia, Italy, and has been around since the 1800s.

Sliced root has alternating white and red rings. It matures in 55 days and should be harvested when the root has a 2-inch diameter.

Detroit red beet is crimson-colored and another heirloom that has been around since the 1890s. Developed by Mr. Reeves of Ontario,

Canada, from Early Blood Turnip beet, it was improved and then marketed by D.M. Ferry seed company in Detroit in their 1892 catalog. Detroit was once the seed production capital of the world, thanks to Dexter Ferry. You can still buy seeds from his company under the name of Ferry-Morse seed packets. He started packaging seeds and selling the packages to general stores, and, voila, the seed rack was born. This beet is deep, deep red, matures in 55 days, ready to harvest, reaching a 3-inch diameter. Beets that you purchase at your local market stand a good chance of being a Detroit Red.

Radish

Radishes are the darlings of the garden. They are easy to grow and ready to harvest in a month. So this is a good vegetable for children to grow. It grows within their gardening attention span.

Belonging to the Brassicaceae family, which is the cabbage family but a different genus, it is a distant cousin of cabbage. The whole plant is edible. Roots are fleshy and crisp, sometimes with a pungent flavor. Leaves can be added to salads or stir-fried, and seed pods add a good crunch to a snack with a beer. We are conditioned to small red round or small white icicle radishes, but in Europe in the 1500s, some radishes weighed as much as 100 pounds. In Asia, radishes are popular as pickles.

History of the plant is thought to have originated in China. There are scant archeological records to pin any area down. Wild forms have been found in China and India. The radishes that Greeks ate and used for medicinal purposes were long, large ones, similar to daikon radishes. Medical properties continued through the Anglo-Saxon era, with it being touted as a remedy for women's chatter, obviously, to no avail. However, the amount of vitamin C is enough to prevent scurvy. The small round radish of today began appearing in the 1500s in Holland and Italy.

The Dutch gave us the ancestor of the white round radish, of which the **Philadelphia White Box** is a variety. Italy gave us the ancestor of the small red round radishes of today. Another shape is the icicle radish, which is finger-shaped and was developed in the 1600s.

It is a biennial, grown as an annual cool weather root. They are divided into two types: summer, which are the small snacking radishes, and winter, which are larger, taking longer to mature.

Summer radishes can be planted as soon as soil can be worked in spring but do poorly when summer temperatures heat up. Plant in full sun, harvesting when radishes are about the size of a large marble.

Winter radishes take longer to mature, around 50 to 60 days. These are typically planted in late summer and harvested before winter takes hold. Plant these in full sun. Harvest size depends on the variety planted. Daikon varieties can weigh several pounds. So, it is important to read your seed packets.

They will germinate in 3 to 4 days, and seeding depth depends on the variety of radishes, from ¼ to ½ inch deep. The important part is to thin the seedlings. Give smaller type radishes at least 1 inch or more between plants. Larger types need 3 to 4 inches between them to develop into their appropriate shape. Seeds need to be directly sowed in loose, well-drained, but moist soil.

Radishes don't transplant well, so sow seeds where they will develop. It is not unusual to see a radish's 'shoulder' at soil level for any variety. Use the size of radish shoulders to determine whether they are ready to be harvested. If left too long in the ground, the roots become woody and tough. I work composted manure in the soil before sowing seeds. Interplant them among peas, lettuce, or carrots. Seeds remain viable for 5 years.

A couple of pests that you need to look for are aphids and cabbage root fly. Aphids are soft-bodied insects that I have mentioned in other chapters. They are opportunistic critters that will invade a range of vegetables.

The cabbage root fly is a small fly that lays eggs at the base of radish, cabbage, turnip, and several other vegetables. The eggs hatch, and larvae are white. They tunnel down into the roots, eating their way to becoming a pupae, which will become an adult fly. Three generations of this process can occur over one growing season. The last generation of pupae will overwinter in the soil, waiting for spring. Now, what do you do? Non-chemical options include placing a floating row cover over the radishes to keep the adult fly from laying eggs. Or rotating the planting area every time you plant in order to starve pupae if present in the soil. What is a floating row cover? It is a thin material of different weights that is spun or bonded and made from different substances, such as plastic or polyester. It lets the sun and moisture in but keeps insects out. It will also help hold heat, protect against frost damage, or help warm the air in early spring.

If you harvest radishes that are split, this is due to uneven watering or waiting too long to harvest them.

For the most part, I don't have too many pests attacking radishes. What I do have is a vegetable that helps shield other vegetables from attack. Radishes produce a scent that is unattractive to some insects. So, interplanting short rows of radishes among peas, melons, carrots, and lettuce will help keep damaging insects away. Plus, it adds eye appeal and texture to the garden. I don't have a boring monoculture of long, straight rows. Some vegetables are planted in rows, while others can be scattered throughout the garden. Radishes are planted in a row because their transplanting survival rate is low. Seed a row, thinning it when seedlings appear.

Plan on leaving some radishes to flower during the summer months. Bees and butterflies will thank you.

The word 'radish' came to us from Middle English, which came from Old English 'raedic.' It is traced back to Latin 'radix,' which means root.

Vitamin C is found in moderate amounts, along with some essential vitamins. It is that wonderful crunch with a pungent flavor that keeps us munching away.

Zlata radish is a summer heirloom from the Slavic states of Eastern Europe. The word means gold, and it is a golden plum-shaped radish with white inner flesh. Sow seeds in early spring as soon as soil can be worked and additional plantings every 3 weeks for a continuous supply until the summer heat takes over. Days to maturity is only 30. Harvest when it is 1 to 2 inches in diameter. This one is slow to bolt or crack.

Mantanghong, or watermelon radish, is a winter-type hybrid. It has a globe-like shape and has green outer skin with a fuchsia-colored inner flesh. With a diameter of at least 3 inches, this radish can weigh close to a pound. It is frost-tolerant and has a mild flavor. Plant this one in late summer for a fall harvest. It needs 60 days to reach maturity.

Pink Beauty is a round pink summer radish that is ready in 26 days. It has a mild taste, is crunchy, and is harvested when it is 1 to 2 inches. It is an heirloom and has white inner flesh. It will germinate in 4 or 5 days. This one does better than others in warmer weather.

Philadelphia White Box radish was listed in the Landreth and Sons catalog in 1890. It is a white, round, winter type that is ready to harvest in 30 days. These are small, about 1 inch in diameter, which makes them a good option for planting in boxes, cold frames, or pots, hence the name box radish. They have a mild flavor and can be planted in spring and fall.

Chapter 10: Summertime Treats

The Cucurbitaceae family is a large group consisting of cucumbers, melons, and watermelons, among others. Geographic origins are all centered in the tropics or subtropics of Asia and Africa. Frost-intolerant annual vines that are grown in the summer months or under protective covers, such as greenhouses in temperate regions of the world.

Some physical characteristics are shared among this large group. Most of the varieties are monoecious, a long word that means the plant has separate male and female flowers. Most of the flowers that are produced at the beginning of a growing season are males. So don't worry when your cucumbers or melons have a lot of flowers at the start of the growing season that don't produce fruit. Females come a little later. The plant knows what it is doing! How do you know the difference? Female or pistillate flowers will have a tiny ovary growing at the base of the flower, which becomes the fruit that you harvest. Male or staminate flowers have a small stem at the base of the flower. The flowers are insect pollinated, so bees will be visiting all of the flowers.

Cucumbers, melons, and watermelons are botanically classified as a berry. A fruit that has many seeds, fleshy pulp, and produced from a single ovary is a berry. These fruits are also classified as pepos. Pepos have all the characteristics of a berry but also have a leathery or hard rind. Just to confuse the issue, strawberries, and raspberries are not true berries.

They have a trailing or vining growth habit with hairy stems, and most plants have tendrils.

Tendrils are modified leaves or stems that curl around an object to support the plant. Vines have limited ability for upright growth. But they are still programmed to grow or move toward a stimulus, which in this instance is light or sun. In the plant world, this is called tropism.

Now, you add auxin, a plant growth hormone found in cells that stimulate cells to elongate. In this case, we are just concentrating on looking at the tips of the shoots. If the sun is directly above a shoot, then the plant goes up because the cells will elongate evenly. If the sun is at an angle, then the shoot bends toward the sun. Why? Auxin moves laterally within the cell away from light to the 'dark' side. There will be an overabundance of auxin on the dark side, which will cause the cell to change its shape. Picture a round cell bending toward light and, in the process, ends up not a round cell but a cell that is a half-moon shape. The outer curve is the dark side, and the inner curve is the light side. So now you have a plant shoot leaning towards a light source.

Why do they curl, and which way do they curl? So far, we have the tendril bending but not forming tight curls. Plants have a sense of touch that is unlike an animal's sense of touch. Those of you who have grown cucumbers, peas, beans, or any other vine will have noticed that the tendril begins to make wide arches or bends. This wide, meandering arching that seems to just go out into thin air will eventually bump into something: another plant, a branch, a support that you have installed, etc. What makes it curl around that object? Once the tendril has touched an object, a signal goes out to a group of cells that have specific purposes. One set of cells begins to exude water, causing it to contract, whereas another set of cells will become rigid or stiff. These two actions cause the tendril to curl tightly.

Which way do they curl? Clockwise or counterclockwise? They curl in both directions.

Look closely at your cucumber tendril and follow it. They will develop a kink and then reverse directions. These tight curls in both directions are very important to anchor and support the weight of the plants.

Cucumbers

Cucumbers are as big a part of summer as tomatoes and beans. Cucumis sativus is an Old World plant with a place of origin thought to be at the foot of the Himalayas in India, and this wild ancestor is bitter. Bitterness is derived from compounds called cucurbitacin. It was a defensive mechanism to ward off pests, which included insects but also grazing animals, including humans. Cultivated for at least 3000 years, today's cucumber has had most of the cucurbitacin bred out.

From the Indus Valley, it traveled east to China and Japan, both countries developing and readily accepting it into their cuisines.

Caravans traveling from central Asia west into Eastern Europe are probably responsible for introducing cucumbers to Europe. Romans adopted and enjoyed cucumbers. In areas of Northern Europe and England that were not conducive to growing cucumbers, forcing of plants was developed. Using cold frames or a form of hothouses allowed cucumbers to be enjoyed year-round. There are records of cultivation in France in the 9th century and England in the 14th century.

Cucumbers were eaten in England and then fell out of favor, being blamed for all sorts of maladies. After consuming them for several centuries, it was decided that cucumbers were poisonous and only good for animal fodder. Samuel Johnson (1709 to 1784) is quoted as saying, "A cucumber should be well sliced, dressed with pepper and vinegar, and then thrown out." It was about this time that cucumbers were referred to as cowcumbers. Good for animal fodder only.

Cucumbers arrived in Hispaniola with Columbus. Spanish explorers introduced them to Native American tribes, and cucumbers were well established when the first colonists arrived in North America.

I start seeds indoors during April, but I also sow seeds directly in the garden in June. Sowing times will vary from region to region and will depend on the individual microclimates of your garden. Sow or plant after the last frost date. Soil temperature needs to be between 65 and 75 F. Air temperature should be between 50 and 95 F. That is a huge range, but the optimum is 75 to 80 F. A sunny location with moist, well-drained soil will help keep cucumbers happy. Cucumbers only need between 50 to 65 growing days to mature and produce. Seeds remain viable for up to 5 years if kept in a cool, dry place, so don't throw out last year's seeds! But do buy different varieties to try from year to year.

Cucumbers are annuals, and most are vines, but there are varieties that have a bush habit due to very, very short vines. Vine cucumbers will respond well to staking and are good candidates for vertical gardening using less space. If you don't want to stake them, then planting on mounds is also an option. Mounding eliminates chances of standing water around the roots. Just remember to give them plenty of sprawling room. I prefer staking to conserve ground space to be used for other vegetables. Keeping plants and fruits vertically eliminates hiding places for insects.

How many times have you reached for a cucumber and found it to be curled? It is fatter at one end, tapering to the other end. This is due to inconsistent watering. After plants are established, then 1 inch of water once a week is sufficient. How do you know? Stick your finger in the soil, and if it is dry up to your first joint, then it needs water. If it is wilted at day's end, then this is usually temporary due to heat. However, if plants are wilted in the morning, they need to be watered. And there is such a thing as over watering which can lead to losing the whole plant.

Two results of eating cucumbers can be a bitter taste and burping. Cucurbitacin is the culprit responsible for both. Breeding has removed most of this compound, but stress during development can result in bitterness reappearing. Some people are more sensitive to a bitter taste than others, so it can depend on an individual's chemistry as to whether bitterness is tasted. This compound is found in the stem end and peel, so cutting off 1 inch of the stem end and peeling cucumbers can help reduce bitterness. Fannie Farmer's 1896 cookbook mentions cutting off the stem end and peeling to remove bitterness, so this method has been around for some time. If still bitter, then peel, slice, and put in a cold water bath with a tablespoon of sugar for a few minutes. This usually reduces the bitter taste.

Burping associated with eating cucumbers results from this same chemical. Higher amounts of cucurbitacin increase the chances of burping. 'Burpless' cucumbers have been bred to have less cucurbitacin. It is not 100% fail-proof.

The plant produces bright yellow flowers that are typically around 1 inch in diameter and have a total of 5 petals. The pollen in the male flower is sticky, so it is not windblown, which necessitates attracting pollinators such as bees. Female flowers are open for only one day, so the bees need to be on the ball.

There are different types of cucumbers, and all are eaten at the immature stage. Slicing cucumbers are smooth-skinned, averaging 8 inches long. Some have thick skins which have had a coating of edible wax applied, which inhibits moisture loss and damage during shipping. Seeds in the standard grocery store cucumber can be large and may need to be removed.

The **Marketmore 76** cucumber is a poster child for slicing cucumbers. Original Marketmore was developed by Dr. Henry Munger at Cornell University in 1968. It is monoecious, with female flowers producing large amounts of fruit, is disease resistant, and has thick dark green skins that help protect it during shipping.

Thin-skinned cucumbers come in different lengths and are typically wrapped in plastic, which serves the same purpose as waxing. You will find them under names such as English, burpless,

Asian, or mini snacking cocktail cucumbers. They are straight with smooth skin in varying shades of green, and seeds typically are small or absent. For best results, grow on a trellis in a protected environment such as a greenhouse or grow tunnels.

In England, they were grown in hothouses or greenhouses. Brits like their cucumbers straight, not curved. Curved ones were fed to the pigs. George Stephenson, a British engineer in the early 1800s, devised a glass tube to slip over a cucumber, keeping it straight. With a combination of a trellis and adequate moisture, the result should give you straight cucumbers, hopefully without glass tubes.

While cruising through a seed catalog, you may come across a cucumber that is described as gynoecious and/or parthenocarpic. Which means what? Gynoecious cucumbers are hybrid cucumbers that have been bred to produce an abundant number of female flowers for high yields. Parthenocarpic cucumbers have been bred to not need a pollinator to produce fruit and have an absence of seeds. These varieties are good candidates for a protected growing environment, and seeds are typically small or absent. I include this here because the majority of English or burpless cucumbers fall under this category.

Sweet Success is an English burpless variety. It is an AAS winner, producing dark green fruits that reach 12 to 24 inches in length. Vines have all female flowers, so no pollinator is necessary.

Suyo Long is an Asian heirloom variety from China. As the name implies, it is long, up to 18 inches. It is tolerant of hot weather but also does well in greenhouses. It is ribbed with dark green skin.

The **Iznik** cucumber is a mini, snack cocktail hybrid. It comes to us from Germany, happily growing outside, under cover, or even in pots. It is a perennial that produces 3 to 4-inch cucumbers on short vines. Practically seedless with smooth, thin skins, they are a perfect snack.

Socrates is a thin-skinned hybrid, sweet and crunchy. It tolerates cool temperatures, which suits my region well. It is parthenocarpic, so it has no seeds, and it will still be produced in lower light conditions in early spring and fall.

Both Iznik and Socrates fall into the category of Beit Alpha cucumbers. The ancestor was developed in the Beit Alfa kibbutz in the 1930s by Hanka Lazarson. These mini snack-size cucumbers are also known as Persian, Mediterranean, or Lebanese. Generally, they are always sweet, crunchy, and never bitter.

Pickling cucumbers are used primarily for processing or pickling, but you can also peel eating them fresh. They have thin skins, short, usually around 4 inches long, fat, and blocky in shape.

They have black spines on their skins that will turn orange as the fruit matures. If a cucumber has orange spines, then it is well past its prime. Gherkins or cornichons are small whole cucumbers that are pickled. They are only one to two inches long and have bumpy skins.

Boston Pickling is an American heirloom that has been around since 1877 and was marketed by the Detroit seed company D.M. Ferry & Co. It has monoecious flowers producing 3 to 7-inch fruits that make great pickles but also are good to eat fresh.

The **Parisian Gherkin** cucumber is a midget heirloom that grows well in pots. It is a hybrid that is a bush-type cucumber reaching just 10 to 12 inches high. It is another AAS winner-producing fruit that can be picked from 1 to 4 inches in length. Just a crunchy little cutie.

Two novelty 'cucumbers' that are not true cucumbers are the

Mexican Sour Gherkin and Armenian cucumber. Seeds for these two are normally found listed with cucumbers from seed companies.

Mexican Sour Gherkin, or **Mouse Melon**, is an heirloom, native from Mexico down to Venezuela and, technically, not a true cucumber. It is a different species but in the same family as cucumbers and is a perennial. It produces 1-inch fruits that resemble doll house size watermelons and are adorable. It is monoecious, having both male and female flowers. It is a great snack raw or can be pickled.

Armenian cucumber has been around since it was cultivated in Armenia in the 1400s. It is not a cucumber but a ribbed melon. Also known as yard-long melon or snake melon, it will mature up to 36 inches long but is best harvested around 12 inches. Has very light green skin, is burpless, and will grow straight if trellised but will twist and turn if grown on the ground. It does well in hot climates.

Cucumbers are a good source of potassium and vitamins K and C. As an added bonus, cucumbers are considered a non-starchy vegetable, which helps control blood sugar levels, and are low in calories if dieting.

The word 'cucumber' comes to us from Middle English, which came from the Middle French word 'cocombre,' which came from the Latin cucumer-cucumis.

The word 'pickle' is from the Middle English 'pikille,' which spans the twelfth to fifteenth centuries. It denotes a solution or bath that preserves or cleans.

The word 'gherkin' comes from Early Middle Dutch 'gurken,' which means small pickled cucumber. This was derived from the

Medieval Greek 'agouros.' Obviously, there was a lot of evolution in the word down through the centuries to end with gherkin.

Cornichons are small pickled cucumbers. Usually no more than 2 inches long and slender, they were incorporated into French cuisine in the 1700s. The word means little horn.

Today the French have their concombre, Italians have their cetriolo, the Spanish have their pepino, Germans have their gurke, and Indian Hindi have kakdi.

'Cool as a cucumber 'phrase has been around for a long time. It implies a person who keeps calm and unemotional in stressful times. Why was cucumber picked as the vegetable to be compared? The interior of a cucumber, even in warm weather, remains up to 20 degrees cooler than the air surrounding it.

The phrase was first put to paper in 1610 in Cupid's Revenge, a play referring to certain women as being cold as cucumbers or emotionally unresponsive to men. I might suggest that this could be due to the idiocy of some men. Be that as it may, the phrase has been around for centuries.

Powdery mildew is the culprit that causes me the most headaches with cucumbers. It is caused by a fungus that can develop in late summer to early fall when moisture is more abundant in the air. A white 'powder' begins to appear on the leaves and spreads quickly. It can also develop if the plants are too tightly placed, which does not allow enough air circulation.

Trellising or staking cucumbers will help with air circulation. Shop for plants or seeds that are labeled 'powdery mildew resistant,' but remember it is not 100% fail-proof. You are dealing with Mother

Nature. You may have to resort to a fungicide. Please read the instructions carefully and weigh your options. Thankfully, my powdery mildew usually shows up at the end of the growing season, so I just pull and dispose of the plants.

Melons

Cucumis melo is a fruit that exists for dessert. You don't need anything else but a slice of sweet melon. In antiquity, melons were not sweet but similar in taste to a cucumber. A variety of sweetless that is still around today is the Armenian cucumber, which is not a cucumber but a melon. Sweet melons are thought to have been present in central Asia in the 9th century. Once again, it falls on the shoulders of Arab conquerors to spread sweet melons west into Europe.

It is an annual vine that needs a warm region full of sun and fertile soil. It is frost intolerant.

Melon taste will be bland until it is ripe, and they will not ripen after harvesting. So, buying a melon that doesn't have much sweetness is a sign that it was harvested too soon. Sweetness in melons is accumulated in the last days of maturity. The sweetest melons are those that have a long period of ripening time. It can be up to 130 days. Regions that have climates that have long, mostly rainless, warm summers, produce the sweetest melons. Flesh color can be salmon, yellow, or green.

Pollination in all Cucurbitaceae members is by bees or insects. Flowers are the plant's reproductive component. The female part is located in the center of a flower called the pistil. Its shape resembles an elongated teardrop, narrow at the top and wider at the bottom. The top has a sticky substance on it, and the wider bottom portion contains the female gametes, which is the ovary. Gametes are reproductive cells that unite with other reproductive cells to produce a fertilized egg, which in the case of plants is a seed, not an egg.

The male half of the equation is called the stigma. It is a filament or flexible stalk with a bulb-shaped tip at the terminal. This bulb tip is called an anther and contains pollen. Male gametes are pollen grains that are sticky and have a rough texture. When the anthers mature, they burst open, pollen is released, and is ready to fertilize. Some plants are self-pollinating, and others, such as cucumbers, melons, and watermelons, need outside help in the form of bees and other insects. Now you know the importance of bees and other pollinating insects. In spring, there is an overabundance of pollen released, which humans experience with allergies and all that yellow dust on your car.

Melons are grouped into several categories. One group is the reticulatus or muskmelon, which has a 'netted rind'; the shape of this melon is lobed and will detach from the vine when ripe.

Confusingly, in the US, muskmelons are referred to as cantaloupes. The word muskmelon is derived from the Persian word musk, which is a perfume describing the fragrance of ripe melons. The second half is melon which works its way back to the Old French 'meloun,' then back to Latin, 'melonem.'

Emerald Gem happened by chance. It was a mutant or natural hybrid from William G. Voorhees' garden in Benzie County, Michigan. The year was 1886, and he sent seeds to Washington Atlee Burpee, and Burpee's seed company put it on the market. An heirloom that develops fruit weighing 2 to 3 pounds, its flesh is a pale orange color that matures between 70 and 91 days.

Fordhook Gem was introduced by the Burpee seed company in 1967. It is a cross between two heirloom varieties, 'Netted Gem' and

'Extra Early Knight.' Fordhook Gem seeds were reintroduced by Seed Savers Exchange in 2021 with a donation of seeds from Amy Goldman.

Ripening between 60 and 80 days, it has green flesh. The rind will develop a yellow glow when ripe.

Minnesota Midget is an heirloom with short 3-foot vines that produce softball-sized melons. Individual servings! It matures in 60 days and is a great one for northern gardens. It was developed by the University of Minnesota and put on the market in 1948. It has sweet orange flesh and does well for those who are gardening in containers.

The second group is cantalupensis, or the true cantaloupes. They are smooth-skinned; some varieties may have warts on their skin. They are also lobed and will detach from the vine when ripe. A story survives that the melon received its name from Cantalupo, a village in Italy that was a papal county seat. A melon was served to the pope and became a favorite.

Prescott Fond Blanc melon is a French heirloom that has been around since the 1880s. Its shape is flattened at the top and bottom with a hard, warty, wrinkled rind. The melon skin is a greenish color that turns to a straw yellow color when ripe. The flesh is salmon colored and weighs between 4 and 9 pounds. This one needs 70 to 80 days to mature.

Charentais melon is another French heirloom from the 1920s in the Poitou-Charentes region of France. Grapefruit or softball in size, it matures in 85 days, weighing about 2 pounds. The rind is thin, which makes it too fragile to ship, so you need to look for one at your farmers' market. It has smooth gray-green skin with darker green stripes and orange or salmon-colored flesh.

A third group is inodorus or winter melons. These have the least fragrance but sweet white or green flesh. The rind will have smooth or somewhat wrinkled skin, is not lobed, and tapers to a slight point at the stem end. It has a thick rind, which makes it a good candidate for shipping and storage, hence the name winter melon. These melons do not detach from the vine when ripe.

Honeydew melon is the third most popular melon in the US. It has a smooth, almost white, thick rind with greenish-white or pale orange flesh. In France, it was known as Melon d'Antibes blanc d'Hiver or White Antibes Winter melon. Its region of origin is southern France and Algeria.

The name honeydew was given by breeder John E. Gauger, who worked for the USDA in Colorado in the early 1900s. An easy, catchy name for Americans that also describes the sweet, juicy flesh found inside. These melons are of large size, weighing between 4 and 8 pounds, needing a long, hot, dry growing season. Most honeydews come from California or Arizona for US markets. Days to maturity range from 70 to 100.

Casaba melons are generally round or acorn-shaped and taper to a point at the stem end. The rind is thick and smooth with lengthwise furrows. It will fade from green to yellow when ripe.

Flesh is white to pale green. Most casabas are grown in southern California or Arizona due to requiring a long, hot, dry growing season, 100 days or more. These melons are thought to have a place of origin in Persia and were introduced to the US in the late 1880s from melons that came from Kasaba, Turkey, hence the name casaba.

A rich source of vitamins A and C, the orange or salmon-colored flesh also contains beta-carotene. However, the most nutritious part of melon and watermelon are the seeds, which are mostly consumed in Africa or China. They are a rich source of protein, fat, calories, thiamine, and riboflavin.

Melons are great with prosciutto or cottage cheese. It is also a refreshing base for fresh fruit salads and smoothies.

Watermelon

If there is a fruit that screams SUMMER, it is watermelon. An Old World vine that comes from Africa. It also has monoecious male and female flowers, along with melons and cucumbers.

Citrullus lanatus is another member of the Cucurbitaceae family, along with cucumbers, but a different genus and species.

Research has concluded its region of origin is northeastern Africa around Egypt and Sudan. It has been on a 5000-year journey, starting as a bitter, tough, water-retaining receptacle to the sweet, juicy summertime treat it is today. Egyptians were cultivating and enjoying them 4000 years ago, leaving depictions of watermelons on wall etchings, but also plant remains found in tombs due to the dryness of the area. Tutankhamun took watermelons with him into the afterlife. Writings in ancient Hebrew, Greek, and Roman literature describe medicinal attributes but also just the pure enjoyment of eating cooling sweet fruit. Wild watermelons can still be found growing in the deserts of Egypt and Sudan.

As with other edible plants, watermelons migrated east and west from their place of origin. The Silk Road is the most likely avenue for watermelons to travel east. Reaching India in the 9th century and finding its way to China in the 10th century. Moors are credited with introducing it to Spain and Italy. The climate around the

Mediterranean coast was conducive to producing watermelons. As the melon migrated to northern Europe, it was grown as a specialty fruit in hothouses arriving in Great Britain in the 16th century.

European settlers and African slaves are credited with watermelon's introduction to the Americas. It was recorded in the early 1600s, and Indigenous Americans were soon planting them.

The word watermelon was first in print in the 1600s. Two words spliced together to describe a melon that contained thirst-quenching water. French have their pasteque, Italians have anguria, Spanish have sandia, and Germans have wassermelone. While only wassermelone is similar in appearance to watermelon, the other three have roots in ancient Arab or Greek.

Zonal Denial is a disease that afflicts all gardeners. Some of you just don't know it. It is planning, contemplating, orchestrating, and otherwise trying to grow a plant that does not fall into your USDA hardiness zone. But…. you do it anyway. The ultimate zonal denial is the ordinary house plant. It is a tropical plant that you maintain in your house for its survival. Watermelon is one of my zonal denial plants. It has no business growing in my cool, wet western Washington garden. But I do it anyway. As expected, yearly results are mixed.

So, what does a watermelon need to grow and produce a sweet, juicy watermelon? It is a warm season crop needing soil temperature around 70 F at planting time. Air temperature needs to be between 70 F and 95 F. Below and above those temperatures, plant growth and maturing of watermelons slows. Soils need to be a good sandy loam that allows air and water circulation and infiltration. Planting in hills is recommended.

And space! If planting just one plant, it will need at least 10 square feet of growing room. If planting in rows, then plants should be spaced 3 to 5 feet apart and row a good 8 feet apart.

They are heavy feeders. I mix in composted manure at the time of transplanting, and then side dress with more manure twice during the growing period. I start seeds indoors in May to transplant out in June for my region. Seeds will germinate in 3 to 10 days. Flesh color ranges from white, cream, yellow, and salmon to red. Research, and you will find one that fits your garden niche.

I have two criteria going against me for growing watermelon: climate and space. To offset this, I plant watermelon that ripens in 70 days, a maximum of 80. There are varieties that have short maturing dates that are great for northern gardens. Choosing a variety that develops a compact plant and produces small melons. I use a lot of straw around the plant to help build and hold soil heat. I choose a seeded variety rather than a seedless one. This eliminates the necessity of planting two different varieties to get a seedless watermelon. Then I cross my fingers, keeping in mind that this is always an experiment in my garden.

What is a seedless watermelon? Developed in the 1930s, they are sterile hybrids produced by two different sets of chromosomes. Watermelon has 22 chromosomes. If a seedling is treated with the chemical colchicine, then that plant will double its chromosomes to 44. Now you have watermelon plants that have 22 chromosomes and some that have 44 chromosomes, each producing flowers. If pollen from the 22-chromosome male flower is used to fertilize a 44-chromosome female flower, then the result is fruit that has 33 chromosomes, which is sterile.

You do find some white 'seeds' in seedless watermelons, but

these are actually just empty seed coats.

How can you grow a seedless watermelon? You purchase a seedless variety, which are seeds from a plant that was treated to develop 44 chromosomes. This plant will still produce male and female flowers, but the pollen from the male flower is not abundant or of good quality. The female flower needs to be pollinated by a regular 22-chromosome male flower. It is a process, and I leave growing seedless watermelons to the experts. If you want to try your hand at producing seedless watermelons, then the seed company will include an additional packet of seeds of a pollinator, and complete growing guidelines to be used. You need to grow two different watermelons and let the bees do the pollinating. Now, you will really appreciate that seedless watermelon!

How do you know if a watermelon is ripe? There are several clues for harvesting. The ground or field spot on the melon will turn from white to yellow. This is the part of the melon that sits on the ground. The vine and leaves are still green, but the tendril (that curlicue) closest to the fruit has turned brown. Also, the melon will change from a bright green to a dull green. If you are purchasing at your local market, then what about the thumping of watermelons? If it sounds hollow, then it is mature and ready to be eaten. If thumping produces a dull sound, it is immature. Watermelons do not continue to ripen after harvesting.

Watermelons contain high amounts of lycopene, which have antioxidant and anti-inflammatory properties. It is low in calories and a good source of magnesium, vitamin C, and B vitamins. Try putting a dash of salt on your watermelon slice. It enhances the flavor.

Blacktail Mountain watermelon was developed by Glenn Drowns in the 1970s. At the time, he lived in northern Idaho, but now he is the owner of the Sand Hill Preservation Center in Iowa. It needs only 70 days to mature, which is great for northern gardens. This is a round melon with red flesh weighing between 6 to 12 pounds.

Sugar Baby Bush watermelon is another early variety that matures in 75 days. It is referred to as a bush melon because vines grow no longer than 3 to 4 feet, which makes it a good candidate for small gardens. It is round, with red flesh, and weighs 6 to 12 pounds with a dark green rind.

Considered an 'icebox' watermelon, it was introduced in 1956. An icebox melon type is a descriptive term, meaning it is small enough to fit in a standard refrigerator.

Desert King watermelon has orange flesh and a pale green rind. It will produce melons weighing 10 to 30 pounds and is drought-tolerant. A good one for southern gardens.

Golden Midget is a miniature 3-pound cutie. This watermelon is so easy to know when it is ripe because it turns yellow. The flesh is a salmon color, and it is sweet. It came to us from two breeders at the University of New Hampshire in 1959. Elwyn Meader and Albert Yaeger kept crossing different varieties until they came up with Golden Midget. All you need for this one is full sun, fertile soil, and 70 frost-free days. You cannot go wrong.

Watermelons pair well with a salty cheese such as crumbled feta. But probably the best recipe for watermelon is a slice of cold watermelon, a hot, sunny, sultry day, and a shade tree.

Chapter 11: Beans Spell Summer

You can truly tell summer has arrived when there are beans in your garden. Beans belong to the legume family, along with peas, alfalfa, clover, lentils, soybeans, tamarind, sweet peas, lupines, lima, and fava, to name just a few. It is a big family. They are the second most important food crop after grasses, such as wheat, rice, maize, and rye.

Phaseolus vulgaris is both a dried bean and a green bean. Dried bean is the mature seed found in a pod. Green bean, also labeled snap bean, is an immature fruit, which is a pod with small seeds.

This common bean is a New World plant, and its region of origin is southern Mexico and Central America. Beans that Columbus was familiar with, such as fava beans, were Old World crops.

New World varieties that he stumbled onto in the Caribbean were very different from ones grown in Europe.

The wild ancestor of the common bean is an annual vine with small seeds within a pod. As the pod matured, it became twisted, popping seeds out for dispersal. Physical changes that evolved on the road to domestication are larger seeds and the loss of this twisting habit. Bush or dwarf-type bean plants followed long after the species had been domesticated. It is hard to pin down when beans were first cultivated. Evidence of bush beans have been discovered in Mexico and dated to around 1000 years ago. Pole beans have been estimated from 6000 years to around 2285 years ago. That's quite a long time span, and discussions continue. Seeds have been found in dry, arid areas of Peru in pre-Columbus graves, so we know that these beans originated in the New World, but the date of domestication is still unclear.

Bean cultivation was known from Argentina to the Saint Lawrence River valleys by the time Champlain, Hudson, De Soto, Cortez, and other explorers came in contact with Indigenous Americans. Captain John Smith and Miles Standish also found Indigenous North Americans cultivating beans. What does this mean? All across North, Central, and South America, indigenous populations have been planting, harvesting, and drying beans for centuries.

In North America, beans, together with maize and squash, were a part of the diet of Indigenous Americans. Planting these three crops ushered in the three sisters phenomenon. This is an intermingling of beans, maize, and squash. Maize offers support for beans; beans have the ability to absorb nitrogen from the air, adding it back into the soil, and squash serves as ground cover. Squash adds mulch and deters animals from eating the beans and maize. Not only did the three sisters complement their growth patterns, but they also complemented the culinary traditions of Indigenous Americans. It was a complete diet. Maize supplied carbohydrates, beans supplied protein, and squash supplied vitamins and minerals that maize and beans did not have.

And as an added bonus, all could be dried and used during winter. This is a classic example of intensive companion planting. It was and is a perfect system.

Explorers took samples of the New World bean back to Europe, and the seeds were consumed as a cooked, dried bean. Then, in the 1600s, something magical happened. One day, a gardener in either France or Italy looked at a small immature bean pod and wondered how it would taste. In all probability, it was most likely a court or royal gardener, not a peasant. Peasants didn't have the luxury of eating anything that had not reached maturity due to starvation always knocking at their door. The next step would have been cooking the green pod and having a court taster try it. Poisoning a monarch is not something you want on a resume. If it poisoned the taster, then wonderment stopped in its tracks. But it didn't, and it was presented to royalty as a special dish. The green bean was born.

So now, let's get down to the business of planting a bean crop and what you need. Beans are an annual summer crop. They complete their life cycle in one season, which is summer. Full sun, preferably for 6 to 8 hours a day, with soil that drains well. You can plant seeds directly in the soil about 1 inch deep and 2 inches apart for bush beans. Wait until after your last frost because the soil needs to warm to a temperature of at least 65F. If you are planting more than one row of beans, remember to leave about 2 feet of space between rows. You need to be able to walk between the rows. If you are planting pole beans that will develop into vines, then you plant 1 inch deep but plant 6 to 8 seeds around a trellis or any support for beans to climb. Now, you wait for the seeds to germinate. This takes about a week.

How much water and fertilizer are needed? When watering, just wet soil and root area, not the whole plant. This cuts down on opportunities for diseases to take hold of above-ground plants.

Check the area around the roots and, if it is dry, then water. If it is still moist, then hold off on watering.

Too much water is an opportunity for root rot. What is this? Root rot is a generic term that describes a pathogen that attacks plant roots. The plant's roots become brown and mushy, and the top of the plant appears to be wilted even though the soil is moist. If this develops then plants need to be dug up and destroyed. Do not replant in the same area.

Beans are 'light feeders.' I mix composted manure into the soil before planting seeds, and this usually carries plants through a growing season.

The Legume family of plants has evolved a means of absorbing nitrogen from the environment and changing it into a usable form. Beans develop root nodules when growing, which are 'bumps' on the roots that you can actually see. Rhizobia bacteria enter root cells and start forming these nodules. The plant supplies nutrients for the bacteria, and in return, this bacteria is taking nitrogen that is in a state that plants can't use, converting it into a state that plants can use. Everyone wins in this relationship.

Beans will have nitrogen in their root nodules but also nitrogen in their stems and leaves. So, at the end of a growing season, I do not pull bean plants out of the ground. I cut them off at the soil level, leave roots in the soil, and bury the rest of the plant. Nitrogen in the plant will decompose and be released back into the soil.

Green beans are ready to harvest 50 to 80 days after planting. If you live in a region with a short growing season, choose a variety that reaches maturity in 50 to 60 days. You don't have to wait too long to start enjoying fresh beans! You need to harvest your green beans frequently, sometimes daily, because harvesting generates more production of beans. I like harvesting green beans when pods are the diameter of a pencil or smaller.

Seeds remain viable for 3 years, so keep those unused seeds for another planting season. Try different varieties from year to year.

The oldest variety of green beans is the string bean. A stringy fiber develops along the pod seam. It is edible but tough. Processing string beans meant that this fiber was pulled from the pod. A common heirloom variety in France, which is available in North America, is the **Fin de Bagnols** string bean. It is a bush bean, ready to harvest in 50 to 60 days, picked small before any strings develop, and considered a gourmet bean.

Americans grew up eating **Kentucky Wonder** beans. Heirloom that was known as Texas Pole, then reintroduced as Kentucky Wonder in 1877. It is a pole bean, so it needs something to climb and is ready to harvest in 65 days. Pods will grow to 8 or 9 inches long; at this point, you will want to remove any string. When picked at only 4 to 5 inches long, strings typically have not developed.

'Modern' green beans are stringless. It has been in existence since the 1890s, developed by Calvin Keeney of Le Roy, New York. Burpee Seed Company acquired a variety from Mr. Keeney and marketed it as **Burpee's Stringless Green Bean** pod in 1894. Still marketed today and is ready to harvest in 55 to 60 days.

Provider is another variety of stringless green beans. It was bred by the USDA Vegetable Breeding Laboratory of South Carolina in 1966. It is a bush bean with straight pods 5 to 6 inches long containing purple seeds. This variety can be planted earlier than others because it will germinate in cooler soils. It is resistant to powdery mildew and mosaic virus. There isn't much to dislike about this bean.

Blue Lake bean can either be a pole or a bush bean. It was developed around the Blue Lake district of California in the early 1900s for canning purposes. Breeders in Oregon took it a step forward, eliminating any strings, producing a smooth, crisp, stringless green bean, and putting a snap in a bean when it is broken. Today, there are multiple varieties of Blue Lake beans. It stands a good chance of being the most popular bean.

Growing beans to be shelled and dried is basically the same procedure. The difference is leaving pods on the vine until the seeds are mature. So… You plant the bean seeds and basically walk away, letting them get on with their mission, except for watering and weeding. You do not pick these bean pods but leave them on the vine. Plants will produce a number of pods and then either stop or severely slow down the production of pods. After seeds enlarge then, the pod will start to dry. This takes a whole growing season. How do you know when these beans are ready to harvest?

Seeds will rattle in the pod. At this point, I shell them, laying the seeds on a flat surface to continue to dry. Then, they are stored in a jar until used. So why would you plant shelling beans when you could just go buy them? Shelling beans out of your garden are meatier than commercial dried beans; they keep their shape even after long cooking times, and they are more flavorful.

Heirloom shelling beans come in a variety of colors and even patterns of several colors. They are beautiful. Some have been lost forever, but some have been grown for generations and are now available to gardeners.

Jacob's Cattle bean is one that has been around since the 1600s, but its known area was only in Southeastern Canada and the Northeastern United States up through the late 1900s. Grown by the Passamaquoddy Tribe, which straddles Maine and New Brunswick, it is a kidney bush bean that is white and maroon in color. It has a rich, nutty flavor and is a good addition to soups or stews. This bean is listed on the Ark of Taste list.

What is the Ark of Taste? It is an international catalog of endangered heritage foods, both plant and animal, which is maintained by the global Slow Food movement. Food that is culturally linked to a region, ethnicity, or traditional production practice. It is a wonderful source of historical data.

Cherokee Trail of Tears bean is a pole bean that can be eaten as a small green bean or left on the plant to produce beautiful, shiny black beans for drying. This bean has been a part of the Cherokee culture dating back before European settlements and was brought to Oklahoma by Cherokees on their death march from the southern Appalachian region, which began in the 1830s. This heirloom matures between 65 to 85 days, depending on whether it will be consumed as a green bean or letting it mature for a dry bean. Vines can grow to eight feet. It is listed on the Ark of Taste list. These seeds have also found their way to the Svalbard Global Seed Vault in Norway. The Cherokee Nation is the first American tribe to send varieties of seeds, preserving a piece of their culture.

What is the Svalbard Global Seed Vault? It is a vault built into the side of a mountain in northern Norway. It holds over 1 million seed varieties from all over the world, safeguarding the immense gene pool of our food sources.

The nutritional value of dried beans is long. It is a good source of plant-based protein, but carbohydrates added with the protein give dry beans a low glycemic index. Soluble and insoluble fiber in dry beans are both beneficial. Soluble fiber helps lower the LDL cholesterol levels, and the insoluble fiber helps keep constipation and colon cancer away. They are high in potassium and iron.

The nutritional value of green beans is just as impressive. High amounts of vitamin K, B2, and C, along with protein and fiber. To retain the most benefits from raw green beans, steaming is recommended. Beware of sodium levels in canned green beans.

The English word 'bean' came to us from Middle English 'bene,' which came from Old English 'bean.' It has been traced back to the Old High German 'bona.' The word is used in a variety of categories: nouns, verbs, and phrases. When used as a noun, it refers to the shape of an object, such as a coffee bean or soybean. It can be used as a verb, such as 'to bean someone on the head,' which means to hit. A number of phrases have developed, such as 'string bean' or 'bean pole' when referring to a tall, thin, lanky person. Someone is 'full of beans,' meaning exuberant. A person didn't 'know beans about it,' meaning they didn't know much or anything about the subject. 'Using the old bean' means using your head or thinking. 'To spill the beans' means to tell a secret. So, if you don't know beans about growing beans, then become full of beans with excitement and use the old bean to grow and harvest a crop of beans!

Chapter 12: Green Pearls of the Garden

Spring wouldn't be spring without peas in a garden. Whether to plant shelling, snow, or snap is always a decision. Seed catalogs start arriving in December. I sit and pore over them. Some catalogs list their seeds with a scant write-up. Other catalogs are almost encyclopedias. I seem to end up in the pea section of seed catalogs first.

Peas are an Old World annual cool weather crop in the Legume family. The ancestry of today's pea is a shelling pea. They have been around for 9000 years, give or take a thousand. Epicenter is thought to cover a rather large geographic area starting in the Middle East, Iran, and extending east into the Inner Asiatic Center, which encompasses northwestern India, Afghanistan to western China.

Domesticated around 8000 years ago, it was grown to maturity and then dried, making peas an easy item to transport and a good food source during winter months.

It was a starchy tough pea, probably boiled into gruel or roasted. What is gruel? Typically, it is a grain such as oat or wheat that is boiled in water or milk. It is a thinner version of porridge.

Peas spread into Western Europe and East Asia, but it was a slow, uneven process. Seeds were taken with clans as they migrated or simply hitchhiked along, hidden in bags of wheat or barley or any numerous other hidden nooks. Climates varied, which in turn helped or hindered the success of pea seeds. Ones that did succeed were nurtured, developing into new varieties in a very primitive process. We still have dried peas today in the form of split peas. It is dried, the outer seed coat is removed, and the pea splits in two.

Enjoyed by Romans, Greeks, and Egyptians, it is the Romans that are credited with introducing them to England during the Roman-British period (AD 43 to 410). The English climate was conducive to pea cultivation. It grew alongside staples of an English Medieval garden, such as the fava or broad bean. This pea was present in all kitchen gardens of all classes, rich and poor. Its redeeming virtue was starchiness, which kept populations alive. The taste of the pea was an afterthought. It made a thick pottage, which is a thick soup, a laborer's or poor man's meal. It was starchy, had no personality, but it did fill stomachs. It got the job done, was dependable, and, when dried, lasted through the winter. Since then, the British have taken peas to new levels of cultivation, introducing new varieties for tenderness and sweetness.

Peas did not exist in North America before the 1500s. Christopher

Columbus brought peas to the Caribbean. Explorers to Canada brought peas to the Montreal region. Peas were recommended in a document associated with English colonists arriving on the Mayflower in the 1600s.

After the 1600s, peas were an essential common garden crop. American varieties started appearing around the early 1800s. Landreth Seed Company, out of Philadelphia, introduced the Early Bush Pea. Landreth Seed Company is the oldest seed company in North America, celebrating 230 years.

Peas that we eat today go by the name English or garden pea. It made its appearance in the fourteenth to fifteenth centuries in Italy and France. Italians are credited with introducing fresh, young, immature green peas rather than mature dried ones. A gift of under-ripe green peas to Louis XIV of France in 1660 started a craze of eating green, fresh, immature peas.

The French gave us petit pois, which are small green peas. A classic French method of cooking peas is with onion and lettuce. A classic British method of cooking peas is with mint. A classic Italian method of cooking peas is with prosciutto. Recipes follow.

Eating fresh or dried peas, then you are eating seeds. How do you know when a shelling pea is ready to be picked? Pea pods should be a good green color, not faded, and filled with seeds. If left too long on the vine, then their color begins to fade, and sugar in the peas converts to starch.

Champion of England pea was introduced by William Fairbeard in the 1840s and is a British heirloom. It can reach heights of 10 feet, with pods containing 8 to 10 peas maturing in 60 to 75 days.

Tall Telephone pea is an American heirloom named in honor of Alexander Graham Bell, reaching heights of 8 feet. Peas are ready for harvesting after 60 days, with pods containing 8 to 10 peas.

Pea vines that reach heights of 6 feet or more will be top-heavy, needing strong support, or they will buckle under winds or rain. Both of these varieties are still available from various seed companies.

Shelling peas have a stiff, tough parchment lining in the pod, so peas need to be shelled. Pea types such as snow peas or snap peas do not have this inner stiff parchment lining. Because the lining is absent, we are able to eat both peas and pods in snow and snap peas. When eating the pea with the pod, you are eating a fruit, not just a seed.

The history of snow peas is a bit unclear, but it is thought to be native to the Mediterranean region and then spread to Western Europe, including the Netherlands. The Dutch are credited with introducing snow peas to China through their trading companies in the latter half of the 1700s. The Chinese adopted snow peas, and the rest is culinary history.

The French gave snow peas the name 'mange tout,' which rolls off your tongue smoother than the English translation of 'eat all.' Which I could envision morphing into 'et al' at some point in time. Snow peas should be picked when they are flat, between 2 to 3 inches long. If a pea has started curling, then it has passed its prime and is developing fiber. **Corne De Belier** is a French heirloom that predates 1860.

Snap peas were developed by Calvin Lamborn of the Gallatin Valley Seed Company in Idaho.

It is a cross between a shelling and a snow pea. It was in the 1950s in Twin Falls, Idaho, that Lamborn was attempting to breed a snow pea that did not curl. He ended up with a snap pea, which is a fat-edible round pod. Harvest snap peas before pods begin to lose their bright green color and peas have formed but have not hardened. Not sure? Then just pick one and eat it. If it measures up to your expectations, then you are on your way to harvesting.

Sugar Snap pea was the first variety introduced in 1979. It is a climber growing to 6 feet tall, so it will need a trellis for support. It will germinate in cold, wet soils, days to maturity are 70, and it will keep producing 3-inch pods all season. This is a pea that is sweet enough to pick and enjoy in the garden, never making it to the kitchen! An All-American Selection winner, producing peas earlier in the season than other varieties, you may need to remove the string or fiber before cooking.

Sugar Ann pea was developed from the Sugar Snap pea. It is a dwarf vine reaching only 2 feet tall, so trellising is an option, making it a good candidate for planting in boxes or pots. Days to maturity are 50, and it produces 2 to 3-inch pods. An All-American Selection winner in 1984, this pea is also one of the earliest to produce in spring.

Magnolia Blossom Tendril is a snap pea bred by Dr. Alan Kapular for its hyper-tendrils. Tendrils are thin, threadlike strands that are modified leaves used by plants to attach to an object for support. Hyper-tendrils are an overabundance of tendrils, and this variety certainly has them. Edible pods are light green in color, displaying purple stripes down the pod when mature.

Tendrils are edible, and adding them to a salad puts a little fluff in your salad with a fresh pea flavor.

All three types, shelling, snow, or snap, need to be trellised, which makes them good candidates for vertical gardening. Using less space, shading some other plants that need it, and less bending over for care or harvesting. However, there are some varieties that are dwarf and do not need to be trellised. They just have very short vines and are able to support themselves. A good dwarf variety is **Tom Thumb**. It was developed in the mid-1850s by Landreth and Sons Seed Company, reaching a height of just 6 to 8 inches and tolerating freezing temperatures.

When you eat just a green pea, then you are eating a seed. When you eat a pea pod, then you are eating a fruit. When you are munching on a pea tendril, then you are eating a modified leaf. You can also eat the tender pea shoots. A pea shoot is the young top portion of a plant, which includes leaves, tendrils, and stems. Harvest a pea shoot when plants are 6 to 8 inches tall; just snip off the top two inches. Last but not least, flowers are edible. All have a sweet pea flavor.

So…. Yes, the entire above-ground pea plant is edible at some stage of its growth. Try the tendrils or shoots because they have a wonderful fresh pea flavor, which is a great way to get a jump on spring. They are a great addition to a salad.

We lived in Tunisia for several years, and while there, I partnered with an acquaintance to start a Girl Scout Troop. Our project was growing vegetables. One of the girls was so surprised to discover that peas did not come from a can. Alice in Wonderland was not alone, opening tiny doors that led to a whole new world.

Planting peas is relatively easy if you don't have jays. Or crows. Or chipmunks. Or squirrels. Or mice. Or rabbits. Medieval peasants grew peas. How mentally challenging can this be? For several years,

I planted directly in the ground. I would wait patiently for something to appear only to finally find a perfectly round hole, little more than the diameter of a pencil, with nothing in it but a seed coat. A seed coat is a paper-thin covering that wraps around seeds, protecting the embryo. This was the calling card left for me to find. One would think that a combination of broad life experiences would be enough to handle germinating peas, but I was wrong.

Instead, I have been reduced to standing in the middle of my garden, threatening an unseen thief. Let the games begin. Laying bird netting over the planted area was my surefire way of keeping thieves away. Thieves don't like to walk on the net. Well, I still found holes. Now, I germinate my peas inside. Soaking them in water overnight and up to 1 or 2 days, changing the water twice a day. This speeds up the germination process, and peas will exhibit a whitetail or embryonic root. Then, I plant them in small pots. I keep them in pots until they are about 2 inches high and have several leaves; then, they are transplanted outside. The birds are no longer interested, but mice might be. I just have to keep my fingers crossed that four-legged thieves can't squeeze through the fencing or pop up out of a hole feasting on the young plants.

If planting seeds directly in the garden, then they need to be planted about 1 inch deep, 2 to 3 inches apart, and in full sun. If planting more than one row, then rows need to be 24 inches apart, and don't forget to trellis. If you don't use all your pea seeds, then keep them because they remain viable for 2 to 3 years if stored in a cool, dry place.

The life cycle is completed in one growing season. Spring and fall are their planting times. They need to go into the ground as soon as the soil can be worked in early spring. Summer heat shuts down the production of peas. Roots require consistent moisture, which is a key factor in producing a continuous supply of pods.

Peas, along with other legumes, have the remarkable ability to take nitrogen from the air and convert it into a plant-usable form. Plants develop nodules on the roots, and these nodules are factories that change nitrogen from a gas form to a soluble form that plants can utilize.

Rhizobium bacteria are the workers in these root nodules that convert nitrogen in exchange for a substance that roots produce, which feeds the bacteria. It is a give-and-take situation. Most nitrogen ends up in the pea or bean that we eat, but there are small amounts that stay in the plant's stems, leaves, and nodules. So what do you do at the end of a growing season to harvest all this nitrogen and put it to good use? I start by cutting pea plants off at the soil level and leaving roots in the ground. Then I take the plant and bury it in the garden. As roots and plant parts decay, they provide nitrogen for other organisms to use.

Our word pea has traveled through several languages. It has its origins in Greek pison, which was translated into Latin pisum. From there, it moved into Old English pise, which became pease. Pease was mistaken for plural, and now we have a singular pea.

Peas are one of the easiest seeds to plant with children. The seeds are big, and soaking them in water allows children to see the beginnings of growth. As peas develop, pods can be picked, shelled, and eaten while in the garden as green Skittles. It is a great way of introducing how a pea should taste.

Harvesting any vegetable, including peas, should be done in the early mornings because they are crispest and juiciest at this time.

During the day, with sun and heat, they tend to lose moisture but regain it during nighttime. Busy schedules often don't allow a perfect picking time, but it is something to strive toward.

Chapter 13: Salad Bowl of Different Colors.

First mention of a zelada or salad was in 15th century Northern Italy. It was more of a salty liquid stew which would be accompanied with a sauce containing pickled greens.

Lettuce was used at this time but cooked in pies or stews. A hundred years later raw greens were chopped, dressed with oil and acid. At this point the word 'salad' was a generic term applied to any individual green or herb.

Romans and Greeks enjoyed an insalata which meant salted things. The 'things' were raw vegetables such as radicchio, arugula, parsley, borage, mint and lettuce but lettuce was not the base of a salad as it is today. It was a wide assortment of greens that added flavor. Salt, an acid such as vinegar, lemon juice, or even brine, and then some oil were added to raw vegetables.

Not too far off what we do today.

Latin 'sal' which means salt is the root word for salad. In Italian it became salata. It became salade in old French and then in 14th century English it became sallet or salad.

Today's use of the word salad encompasses an infinite mixture of different ingredients. There are so many leaves or greens used to create salads. It is endless. Here are a few.

Lettuce

It is probably the most popular edible leaf forming the foundation for so many salads. It is an Old World annual or biennial belonging to the Asteraceae or sunflower family originating in the Caucasus region between the Black Sea and the Caspian Sea. Wild lettuce is bitter, still grows today and it looks similar to a dandelion leaf.

The path to domestication started about 6000 years ago from a plant that produced seeds for oil to a plant of leafy greens that we know today. We know that it had a place in ancient Egyptian culture from wall paintings dating to around 5000 years ago. An upright lettuce similar to romaine, it had a stiff stem and milky sap which had sexual connotations. It was incorporated in their religious rituals and associated with the god of fertility Min. Egyptians pressed lettuce seeds for oil using it for cooking and medication. Lettuce oil is still available today.

Greeks learned from Egyptians and used lettuce as an aphrodisiac but also as a sedative.

Knowledge was passed from Greeks to Romans who served

lettuce salads before the main meal.

Romans ate only the very young lettuce leaves raw and the rest were cooked similarly to preparing spinach.

Romans made a salad of lettuce leaves and a dressing of hot oil and vinegar which was poured over the lettuce. This mixture would have wilted the lettuce. Growing up we always had wilted salads with bacon. My paternal grandmother always had a garden and we waited for that first lettuce harvest of the season. The oil that she used was bacon drippings. Enduring the depression and dust bowl days, she didn't waste anything. Warm wilted lettuce salads have been around for centuries.

Romans took lettuce seeds with them on their march through Europe with a final destination of Britain in 43 AD. Lettuce made its way to China between the 5th and 7th century but it is unclear how it got there. Today China is a top producer of lettuce worldwide. Columbus brought lettuce seeds, among other vegetable seeds, with him on his 1493 second voyage to Espanola in present day Haiti and Dominican Republic.

In the 16th century, Spanish priests, soldiers and explorers brought vegetable seeds which included lettuce to Southeast present day Florida. Lettuce was well established in Thomas Jefferson's vegetable garden in the 1770's.

Today, tucked away in the Svalbard Seed Vault there are 4,000 lettuce varieties. Svalbard Global Seed Vault is located on the Svalbard archipelago between Norway and the North Pole. It is a room chiseled into the side of a mountain that houses over half a billion seeds. Varieties of crops from around the world are kept on ice as a safeguard against catastrophes and climate change.

Romans gave it the name lactuca because of milky natural latex that oozes from the stem. So from Latin lactuca we have English lettuce, French laitue, Spanish lechuga and Italian lattuca. Eastern European countries along with Germany use some form of salat for lettuce.

There are five types of lettuce and dozens and dozens of varieties. Oldest cultivated type is an upright conical shape with long oval stiff leaves. This is Romaine or Cos type lettuce. In the late 1300's, the papal office was relocated to Avignon, France from Italy. Lettuce seeds were brought from Italy and in France it became known as the Roman lettuce hence the name romaine. In Britain, it goes by cos lettuce. This has been attributed to a belief that it originated on the island of Kos off today's Turkey. Another theory is a corruption of the Arabic word for lettuce 'khus'. Because this lettuce has a stiff center rib and is oval in shape it has been used as an edible spoon. A good example of this is the custom of scooping tabbouleh with a leaf of romaine. It is the lettuce of choice in Mediterranean countries. And, of course, a Caesar salad couldn't exist without romaine.

Parris Island romaine is named after Parris Island off the coast of South Carolina. Developed by the USDA and Clemson University it was introduced by the Ferry Morse seed company in

1952. An upright, vase shaped, heirloom lettuce reaching 12 inches in height, it is ready to harvest in 25 to 60 days depending on the size you want.

Crisp Mint Romaine was introduced by the British seed company Thompson and Morgan in 1978. Leaves resemble mint in color and appearance but not flavor. It reaches a height of 10 inches and is ready to harvest in 55 days.

Forellenschluss has its origin in Austria. The name translates to 'speckled trout'. Leaves are green with red splotches. It reaches a height of 8 to 12 inches and is ready to harvest in 55 days.

Solar Flare is a semi-romaine bred by Dr. William Woys Weaver. It is carmen red with slightly ruffled leaves that are full of antioxidants. It grows more upright than spreading and reaches a height of 8 to 10 inches. It adds wonderful color to the garden in summer ready to harvest in 70 days.

Second type is crisphead which is a tightly formed head lettuce sometimes referred to as a cabbage lettuce. A variety was developed from a Batavia lettuce in 1894 by Burpee Seed Company. Farmers in Salinas Valley California had the right soil, climate and precipitation, but they just needed to figure out how to ship it back east. In the 1920's it was packed in ice and sent to the east coast by rail. It became known as Iceberg lettuce. During the 1940's and 1950's that was just about the only lettuce that anyone could buy unless you had a garden. The reason being that it was the only lettuce that could survive cross country shipping. As with all vegetables, it consists mostly of water, it has the least nutritional value and a neutral flavor. To make matters worse, it has been nicknamed 'polyester' of lettuce. But, it has a wonderful crunch and sometimes you just need that crunch as a reward for getting through the day.

The **Igloo** variety has frilly leaf edges and holds well in summer heat, reaching 10 inches in height and width. It produces a size that you are accustomed to purchasing at local food stores. It is crisp, crunchy and ready to harvest in 70 days.

Calmar is another iceberg type that is heat tolerant. Developed at the University of California, it has gorgeous deep green leaves with frilly edges. It is ready to harvest in 75 days and has been around since the 1960's.

Third type is butterhead lettuce, also referred to as Bibb lettuce. They form loose heads of leaves not as tight as crispheads. They are tender and have a buttery flavor. Bibb lettuce is attributed to Mr. John Bibb, a 1812 war veteran in Kentucky. It was originally known as 'limestone lettuce' because it grew well in limestone soils in Kentucky. Mr. Bibb started sharing his lettuce with neighbors and the name stuck as a tribute. It is ready to harvest in 75 days.

Tennis Ball was always found growing in Thomas Jefferson's garden and has come down through the years being mentioned in the Fannie Farmer CookBook of 1896. An heirloom, it is listed in the Slow Food USA Ark of Taste. It produces a head with loose leaves and is petite, reaching just 4 to 6 inches across, it is ready to harvest in 50 days.

Grandma Hadley's lettuce has green leaves that are tinged with dark purple on the margins.

Its name conjures up a crackling fire and comfort food. An heirloom from the 1800's, seeds were saved and handed down at least 4 generations. Seed Savers Exchange acquired some seeds and has put this lettuce back on the market. It is ready to harvest in 40 to 55 days.

Flashy Butter Oak is lime green with splashes of magenta on lobed leaves. Some lettuces are described as 'oak leaf' because leaves are lobed mimicking an actual oak leaf. Bred by Frank Morton at Wild Garden Seed in Oregon it is crisp, buttery and ready to harvest in 55 days.

Winter Density is categorized as a Butterhead-Romaine type. It is dark green with curled leaves that stand up to some heat but is also cold tolerant. This is a good one to plant late summer through fall. It is ready to harvest in 55 days.

Sanguine Ameliore is a French heirloom that was introduced to the American market in 1907 by C.C.Morse Company under the name Strawberry Cabbage lettuce. Center interior leaves are a creamy yellow while outer leaves are green. All are splashed with red throughout. This one can be sowed all winter in milder winter regions. It is ready to harvest in 60 days.

Landis Winter is another that can survive some regional winter weather. It descended from a variety that is now extinct from the 1700's. It is frost resistant. Smooth deep green round leaves have been known to be harvested with snow on the ground. So, days to harvest are basically until you can't wait any longer for fresh lettuce!

Fourth type is loose leaf lettuce. It does not form a head, is probably easiest to grow and most popular. It comes in greens or reds or combinations of both. One advantage of loose leaf is opting to harvest several outer leaves instead of a whole plant. Gently snip off outer leaves and plants will continue to grow. Once it has reached maturity, then harvest the entire plant to keep it from bolting and turning bitter.

Slobolt was developed in 1940's USDA Agricultural Research Center in Beltsville, Maryland.

Light green frilly, leaves are slow to bolt so it will produce all summer. Harvesting starts in 45 days.

Black Seeded Simpson has been a standard loose leaf lettuce.

Bred by Henderson Seed Company in 1875, it has been in gardens ever since. An heirloom of green frilly leaves is ready to harvest in 50 days.

Midnight Ruffles is one of the darkest red varieties of lettuce. Bred in Oregon, it is a rich burgundy almost black in color. It is slow to bolt, heat tolerant and ready to harvest in 45 days.

Speckled is a Dutch heirloom brought to Ontario in 1799. It has smooth round leaves that are splashed with burgundy and ready to harvest in 45 days.

Fifth type is the Batavia, Summer Crisp, or French Crisp type. You will find this lettuce under any of those names. It is a leaf lettuce with tightly spaced leaves, edges or margins of leaves are wavy and the leaf itself is crinkly and crunchy. If left to maturity a head will form. It is somewhat in between a loose leaf and crisphead.

Cherokee has deep red leaves, slow to bolt and resist downy mildew. It is ready to harvest in 45 days.

Anuenue was introduced in 1987 from the University of Hawaii. The name means rainbow.

Green leaves have a slow growth pattern so it stays compact forming a tight heart. It is somewhat winter hardy with some protection, heat tolerant, and ready to harvest anywhere between 30 and 70 days. Harvesting times just depend on your size preference.

One more to add to the list. Musclum. It originated in Provence, France. Farmers would bring a mixture of small young greens to market. Original mixture included leaf lettuce, endive, arugula and chervil. Today, the sky's the limit on what to mix and the percentage of each component. Chard, kale, spinach, radicchio, lettuces, arugula, endive, orach, beet greens, collard greens, watercress, and on and on. They all just need to be small. Create your own.

What is the milky white substance that oozes out of lettuce ribs when broken? It is a lactucarium which is a natural latex. Before Victorian times wild lettuce was harvested and lactucarium was extracted. It was used as a sedative and painkiller. You can purchase bottles of wild lettuce extract today. Today's varieties of garden lettuce have harmless amounts of lactucarium and eating a caesar salad will not put you to sleep.

As plants mature a bitter taste will develop. To solve this problem of bitterness, water frequently and pick when plants are young before it bolts or flowers. What is bolting? When plants have reached a stage in their maturity and temperature and light amounts have changed, then plants will send up a stalk which will produce flowers and then seeds. Another term used is 'going to seed'. The plant is more than happy to do this, you may not be as happy.

Lettuce has to be the easiest vegetable to grow. It is considered a cool season crop, but there are varieties now that resist bolting in summer's heat and some that are winter hardy. It can be directly seeded but also can be sown in seed trays and then transplanted to the garden.

Lettuce is considered a heavy feeder which means it needs fertile soil. When I sow seeds I first use a hand rake to work in some composted manure lightly turning and 'fluffing' the soil. Then I smooth the area. Sprinkle lettuce seeds in a row or just scatter them, barely cover with additional soil and lightly press this area with my hand. Lettuce seeds need to be planted only ⅛ inch deep and by following these instructions seeds will end up ⅛ inch deep. The reason for planting on soil surface and then barely covering is an important depth requirement.

It is also important not to let this area become dry. How many of you have planted a row of lettuce seeds and absolutely nothing comes up? It's OK, you can raise your hand because we have all been there. Seeds were not kept moist enough once planted or were planted too deep and were never going to see the light of day. One more reason is the seed lost its viability. Seeds kept in a cool dry area should remain viable for 5 years.

When starting seeds in a seed tray fill units ¾ full with soil that is recommended for seedlings. Then wet the soil. Lay a few seeds on top of soil, sprinkle some more soil over seeds, press down gently and lay some kitchen plastic wrap over the seed tray. Plastic wrap acts as a small greenhouse and you may not need to water again until after germination. Lettuce seeds germinate quickly, usually within two to twelve days. At this point they need to be moved to a south facing window, placed outside in a sunny spot or under a grow lamp.

Lettuce transplants happily and once plants are big enough to handle then I plant them in the garden. If plants are spaced too close together, you could be encouraging slug issues. So leave several inches between plantings. You can thin them as they grow, adding them to your nightly salad. Soil temperature of 40F or higher is adequate for germination.

Lettuce does best when the air temperature is between 45F to 65F which makes it a cool season crop. It also needs a minimum of six hours of sun. Roots are shallow so adequate watering is important. Days to maturity for lettuce range from 45 to 70 days. So your time and effort will have a short turnaround before enjoying fresh lettuce.

A good source of vitamin A and potassium with the darkest leaves having most nutrients. As with most vegetables, lettuce is mostly water at around 95%.

It does have its pests. My major pest in the Pacific Northwest region is the slug. To discourage them I lay a good layer of straw around the lettuce rows. Most of the time it works. If I find a slug I pick it off, sending it to slug heaven. Aphids, cutworms and other types of worms can also do damage. It varies from region to region. Check your local Extension Office or State University Education websites for help.

Spinach

Spinach adds a deep cucumber skin green to your salad. It is an Old World annual crop and thought to have originated in the region of Persia/Nepal. Spinach is a member of the Amaranthaceae family of plants which also includes beets and chard along with a host of ornamentals.

Our word spinach comes down from Persian 'aspanakh' which wound its way through Arabic 'isbanakh' into Old Spanish Catalan 'espinac', into Modern French 'epinard', and finally Anglo French 'spinache'. Words travel as far and wide as seeds. What an amazing twist and turn through time and geography.

Today's spinach varieties have developed from Spinacia tetranda. This is the wild ancestor that still grows and is gathered in Turkey. It traveled to the Far East several hundreds of years before it traveled west into Europe. The Chinese happily incorporated it into their diet and gave it the name Persian vegetable or Persian green.

Spinach is one of many new vegetables that conquering Arabs

brought into the Mediterranean region. Known in 11th century Spain and 13th century Italy, spinach was grown by Arab farmers and slowly became incorporated into the local food system. Islamic cuisines developed an important relationship between the color of food and its meaning. Green from spinach and other greens signified birth. Christian cuisines also held important significance to food color. Green was the color of Epiphany and fertility. Spinach traveled, finding its way to France and England in the 14th century.

There is a myth or story that Catherine de Medici brought spinach among other vegetables and customs with her when she wed future French King Henry the 2nd. She was born in Florence and was only 13 ½ years old when she wed becoming his queen in the 16th century. A thirteen year old who liked spinach. That is one for the records!

What is known is that royalty traveled with a complete household including cooks. So it is more likely that when Catherine left Florence for France all sorts of articles which could have included seeds were packed. It would have included an entire entourage for her comfort and to bring a little bit of home with her. When Florentine recipes were introduced in France that included spinach they became known as dishes a la Florentine. So, today we have recipes that are 'a la Florentine' which means it is served on a bed of spinach or has spinach incorporated in the dish thanks to Catherine de Medici's cooks.

Spinach finds its place among foods that are either loved or hated. It has been called everything from 'prince of vegetables' to a 'watery, tasteless and boiled to a pulp mess which might have a place in a sick man's diet'. Whoever wrote that description definitely had issues with spinach. Our Founding Fathers planted spinach so it was present in North America in the mid 1700's.

In 1824 Mary Randolph published 'The Virginia Housewife Or, Methodical Cook'. It is the first American cookbook which included a spinach recipe. Her recipe called for boiling spinach and then adding butter, salt and pepper. It can't get much simpler than that.

It is a cool weather crop best grown in early spring and fall. Sow seeds directly in the garden for best results. Germination takes around one to two weeks depending on soil temperature and moisture. I use a hand rake to work soil incorporating composted manure into the soil. Smooth surface for planting. Seeds need to be ½ inch deep so I make a furrow or small trench about a foot or two long. I have four of these furrows five or six inches apart so I end up with four short rows. At harvest, it will be a rectangle shape of adequately spaced spinach which is a good example of intensive gardening technique. Intensive gardening is planting close together to maximize space but you do need to leave enough room for air circulation. I harvest all of it, which is enough for one meal. Days to maturity for spinach ranges from 35 to 50. Soil needs to remain moist but not water logged and plants need full sun.

Spinach seeds remain viable for 5 years. It is a good source of vitamin A and iron. However, iron found in spinach is not easily absorbed by the body due to oxalic acid which is also found in spinach. This acid inhibits absorption of iron so to solve this, eat spinach in combination with vegetables with vitamin C. Examples are strawberries, oranges, potatoes or peppers to name a few.

Spinach has some of the usual culprits of pests and diseases. One pest is aphids, which are soft bodied insects. If just a few leaves are infected, then cut those leaves and throw them away. If aphids are extensive then spray with soapy water or canola oil. I usually have a slug or two that have found their way to spinach. I pluck them and squash them. Done. I try not to use chemicals because I don't want to kill the beneficial insects that I need.

There are fungi or mold that can find a home on your spinach. It is one plant living on another and you are the unhappy recipient. Keep adequate space between plants for air circulation.

Morning watering allows leaves to dry during the day. This will help keep leaves free from fungi or mold. Pests and diseases differ from region to region so do some research. I have to say that most of the time I don't have problems. I may have jinxed myself.

There are three types of spinach. Difference is in the leaf. Crinkly, curly dark green leaves are the savoy type. **Bloomsdale** is a savoy type. This heirloom variety was developed in 1826 by David Landreth of Landreth Seeds Company. It was named after the company farm in Bristol Pennsylvania. It is probably the most common spinach seed packet on a seed rack. Days to maturity are 50.

Second type is a flat smooth leaf. It is easier to clean than savoy and **Seaside** is a good example. This is a hybrid, matures in 30 days and is resistant to powdery mildew. Good choice.

Third type is semi-savoy. It just doesn't fit into savoy or smooth and is in between.

Kookaburra is a good representative. This one is also a hybrid, matures in 26 days and is resistant to powdery mildew. All have the same requirements but some have different planting or harvesting times. Again do your research for your area.

Chard

An Old World biennial, chard belongs to the Amaranthaceae

family of plants along with spinach. Beta vulgaris is the same genus and species as garden beets but a different variety. Chard is considered to be the beet's ancestor and has been around for several thousand years. Its place of origin is thought to be the Mediterranean region, it is a leaf beet that does not develop an edible root. Ancient Romans and Greeks knew chard. Greeks are credited with cultivating chard resulting in different colors. It has been present in Europe since written records were kept. A cold, hardy crop, chard gives you something to harvest after summer. It is high in vitamins A, K and C.

This plant probably has more names than any and it is all confusing. In America it is known as chard or Swiss chard. It is not native to Switzerland but it is thought that a Swiss botanist described the plant and somehow it became known as Swiss chard. The word chard comes to us from 14th century French 'carde' which meant artichoke. The British refer to it as Swiss chard, sea kale beet or leaf beet. Romans called the plant beta, in Arabic it is selg which became acelga in Spanish. French is biette and Italian is bietola. It's enough to give you a headache.

Stalks can be some gorgeous colors or just white with shiny green leaves. Chard is a cool weather crop that matures in 50 to 60 days. Plant directly in soil in spring as soon as the ground can be worked. Moist soil with good drainage is a must. I plant seeds in a shallow furrow ½ inch deep. Seedlings pop up after a week. As plants grow I thin them to give enough room for growth also allowing for air circulation. In cool climates chard needs full sun but in areas that experience hot summers then plant some in areas that are partially shaded. I work composted manure into soil before planting seeds.

Harvesting chard is a 'cut and come again' process. Cut enough for your meal but leave the plant. It will continue to develop more leaves. You can harvest small leaves for salad or harvest large leaves to cook. Cooked chard is similar to spinach and can be used interchangeably.

Seeds can be saved for 4 years if kept in a cool dry place. For the most part it is an easy care plant. Pests, if they should show up, are typically aphids or leaf minors. Powdery mildew might develop if the plant is constantly wet.

Ruby Red, sometimes referred to as Rhubarb chard, has been around since the 1850's. It was first grown as a curiosity, then after the Civil War its popularity grew as a nutritious green.

Stems are a candy apple red with dark green leaves.

Bright Yellow chard has bright happy yellow stems with deep green leaves.

Fordhook chard has white stems with deep green leaves. It was introduced in 1924 by the Burpee Seed Company and it is bolt resistant.

Bright Lights chard is a mixture of colored stems with deep green leaves. Johnny's Selected Seeds acquired seeds developed by breeder John Eaton of New Zealand. It was awarded the All American Selections winner in 1998. All chards add a colorful addition to a garden and all mature between 30 and 60 days depending on the size of leaf that you want.

Perpetual Spinach is a heirloom chard that has been around since the 1800's originating in England. As its name implies, leaves resemble spinach and are a good substitute for spinach. It lasts through warm summer months, tastes similar to spinach and is slow to bolt unlike spinach. It matures in 50 days.

Arugula

Last to an abbreviated list of greens is arugula (Eruca vesicaria). It is an annual Old World crop native to the eastern Mediterranean region and belongs to the Brassicaceae family with cabbages. It is a distant cousin of cabbage. A mainstay in Italy since Roman times.

One of its reported attributes is a stimulant or aphrodisiac. For a period of time it was forbidden to plant arugula in monastic gardens. Then it was decided that, yes, you could eat arugula, but it was mixed with lettuce in a salad. Arugula stimulated you and lettuce calmed you. So the net result should have been an emotional void. It has a bitter, tart peppery taste. It is packed with amazing amounts of calcium and vitamins C and K.

In England, Australia and New Zealand it is called rocket, rucola in Italian from where Americans get our word arugula, roquette in French and gargir in Arabic. It is found just about everywhere in the world today. It is very easy to grow, does well in partially shaded areas and reseeds itself without a second thought.

Plant seeds directly in the garden. It is a cool weather crop that is happy being one of the first in spring. Soil temperatures need to be 45F to 50F and air temperature between 45F to 75F. Germination takes 7 to 10 days. You will be harvesting arugula 30 to 40 days later. It will tolerate a light frost, needs full sun, but in warmer climates, plant in partial shade to protect it from excessive heat. I work composted manure in the area before planting and soil needs to remain moist.

Seeds remain viable for 4 years. There are few pests and diseases. Watch for aphids and space plants for air circulation to reduce the risks of molds developing. And, as with every vegetable, rotate the planting areas from year to year.

One final thought on pests that apply to all greens. We all have native rabbits. And they love vegetables, especially greens. My garden is fenced with what I thought was rabbit proof gauge fencing. I have stood in my garden watching a young rabbit suck in its bones and squeeze out of the garden. I realize that sucking in your bones is not a scientific term but I am here to tell you that it can and does happen. So I have attached bird netting outside of my garden fence about 3 feet high. It seems to work. Rabbits are adorable as long as they are outside the garden and viewed from a distance.

Want to add something out of the ordinary to your salad mix? Here are two edible 'weeds'.

How do plants find themselves relegated to the weed column? Some unfortunate plants even go one step further and find themselves on the noxious weed list in certain states. The concept of a weed is a plant that is not yet held in high esteem, grows where it is not wanted, or is hard to manage. It is an artificial mental concept that humans developed to label some plants.

Dandelion

Dandelion is a member of the Asteraceae family which is commonly referred to as the sunflower or daisy family. It is a perennial herb with every part of the plant being edible. Not native to the Americas, it was brought here intentionally for food and medicinal remedies. The name is a corruption of French 'dent de lion' or lion's tooth referring to the shape of its leaves. It has a tap root which can extend up to 15 feet but most have tap roots 6 to 12 inches. Which explains the excessive amount of digging to try to get all of the tap root with little success.

Young tender leaves can be added to salads. Beer and wine have been made from leaves. A mild diuretic is one of the medicinal qualities. Bright yellow flowers in early spring are a feast for hungry bees. Pulling the yellow petals from the green base can be added to salads as well. The plant is high in vitamins A, C and K with substantial amounts of minerals such as calcium, magnesium and iron.

Along with finding itself on the weed list, it is also on the 'legume oublie' or forgotten vegetable list. Dandelions are here to stay and if the sight of them makes you crazy then just keep mowing them. Pouring chemicals on your lawn is not a permanent fix and in the process you are killing a host of beneficial critters that reside in your soil that you need.

Purslane

Portulaca oleracea is found in every state, Mexico, Canada and everywhere else in the world. Chances are it is growing in your flower bed, in a gravel driveway, in a ditch alongside a road, a cultivated field or any other disturbed piece of earth. You may not know the name of it but it is there. Place of origin is thought to be somewhere in North Africa or the Middle East. It was present in North America before Columbus arrived. Used as a food source for over 4000 years, the stems and leaves have a tart and salty taste when raw.

Purslane is a low growing annual succulent. What is a succulent? Any plant that is drought tolerant and has developed storage tissue for holding water. This tissue can be in leaves, stems or roots resulting in thick fleshy plant parts.

Purslane hugs the soil surface forming a mat of reddish hued stems and fat thick leaves. It produces yellow flowers that some pollinators will visit but the flowers also self pollinate. Plants are high in omega 3 fatty acids, vitamins A and C as well as several minerals.

Chapter 14: The Vegetable's Answer to the Sponge

Eggplant belongs to the same family as tomatoes and peppers. It is an Old World perennial tropical bush but it is grown as an annual. The Nightshade family of plants has a long history of negative myths and eggplant has its share. It was thought to be poisonous, cause insanity or an aphrodisiac which can be one and the same. It was used for medicinal purposes. Touting promises of curing toothaches, intestinal hemorrhages and ear diseases.

John Gerard, a British botanist in the Elizabethan era, advised his fellow countrymen to stick to good ole British fare. It was best to leave eggplant as a garden ornamental plant for pleasure because of its mischievous qualities. He did acknowledge that eggplant was eaten by Africans and Moors in Spain. So Africans and Arabs could withstand the mischievous qualities but the British could not.

It is classified as a berry, 93% water and by itself has nominal nutritional value. Botanically a berry is a fleshy fruit without a stone seed but with multiple soft seeds. There is a long list of fruits that are classified as berries along with eggplant. Bananas, tomatoes, cucumber and pumpkin to name a few. Most vegetables and fruits are 90% water or more and eggplant is no exception.

I start seeds indoors in March. They need 1 to 3 weeks to germinate. After they are about two inches tall, I move them out to a small unheated greenhouse usually late April or May in our region. Eggplant is frost intolerant so you need to be past your last frost date before actually planting in the garden. I reserve the sunniest, hottest spot on our property for eggplants.

Soil temperature needs to be 65 to 70 F before planting. Eggplants will not grow in cool soil. In my region that means putting out eggplants in June spreading straw around eggplants to help keep heat in the soil. Another option for cool areas is to plant in pots in a sunny spot. Pots keep the soil warm and a south facing deck is perfect. It is one of my favorites to grow even though it demands a lot from our region.

Daytime air temperature needs to be between 70 to 85F. When daytime temperatures reach 95F or higher, the plant stops setting fruit and flowers may fall off. If night time temperatures fall below 60 F, then fruit setting is also suspended. In my neck of the woods, it can happen even on a July evening.

Eggplants are considered heavy feeders. I add composted manure before planting, then I sidedress more manure into the soil when plants are about half their mature size. Sidedressing is just working fertilizer into the soil 4 to 10 inches out from the main stem depending on the size of the plant. I fertilize in a circle around eggplants.

I need varieties that have a short growing season for my area.

Short growing season for me is 75 to 80 days max and I have to keep my fingers crossed. Having stated all conditions for having eggplant in your garden; eggplant is easy to grow. Really.

One deadly disease that can afflict eggplants is Fusarium wilt. This is a fungus that lives in soil and enters into the plant's vascular system through root cells. Plants will look limp as if it needs to be watered but soil is damp and has been for some time. You need to destroy the plant by burning or have it hauled away with your trash. Never put it in a compost pile. This fungus will just continue to produce spores spreading in your compost pile. These spores can survive in soil for years. Use this infected area for planting onions or leeks for several years turning your soil in the fall to expose for wintering freezing. This isn't anything to take lightly.

Flea beetle is a nuisance that enjoys chewing holes in leaves of several host plants and eggplant seems to be a favorite. They are small, ⅛ inch or shorter, and come in a variety of colors including black, metallic gray or bronze. They jump from leaf to leaf. While not killing the plant they will stunt its growth delaying the plant's production of fruit. They are most active in spring when plants are small. Putting yellow sticky traps in the garden in spring will let you know if they are present. The beetle overwinters in leaf litter or other sheltered nooks. So I am on guard in the spring looking for holes in leaves. I use an insecticidal soap for control which takes several applications. I use less harmful controls leaving pesticides to the end if all else fails.

Eggplant's place of origin is not conclusive. It has been cultivated in India and China for 1500 years. Archaeological evidence is lacking. Sanskrit and Chinese literature has been relied on to help trace its origin. It found its way east with help from Arab traders on the Silk

Road. Arabs brought eggplant to Persia and from there it spread to Africa. It traveled west to Spain again by Arabs who settled there and from there it spread into Europe. Spaniards are responsible for bringing eggplant to the Americas.

As the plant migrated along the Silk Road its name began to morph into a wide assortment of names. Today names are just about as numerous as seed varieties. Every region of the world has a name for it.

Most are derived from a root word 'vatin-gana' in the Indic language. Persians borrowed it and it became badingan. Then Arabs borrowed it and it became al-badinjan. Arabs or Moors settled in Spain and some European names today have their root word in Arabic. Spanish is la berenjena which became aubergine in French.

The English word 'eggplant 'is derived from the fruit that found its way to England in the 1500's. It was egg shaped, white or yellow about the size of a swan's egg. It was grown as an ornamental plant, still available today and is just cute enough for young gardeners to be interested. Purple eggplants arrived much later.

Italian melanzane was borrowed from Greek melitzana who borrowed it from Arabic.

Melanzane translates to 'mad apple'. At one time eating this fruit was thought to cause madness which explains the 'mad'. Centuries ago the word 'apple' was applied to anything that was unknown. There just wasn't an appropriate name so several vegetables were given the name 'apple' including tomatoes and potatoes.

In India, it is brinjal and considered the king of all vegetables. The Portuguese had trade routes and colonies on the Indian continent and

SE Asia. As a consequence the name brinjal changed in other countries. In Portugal it is berinjela.

Terong is the name for eggplant in most Indonesian countries. Varieties are long and are used for stuffing or replacing pork in recipes for Muslims.

Varieties of tomatoes and peppers have exploded in North America but varieties of eggplant have lagged behind. Just look at selections of tomatoes and peppers at a vegetable stand compared to the usually one or two varieties of eggplant. One always present is a Black Beauty variety.

Black Beauty is an heirloom that was introduced by Burpee Seed Company in the US and has been around for 100 years. Seeds germinate in 1 to 2 weeks in full sun. It takes 75 days to mature, producing black purple fruits. Just a good all around eggplant.

Little Fingers eggplant is the size of... well your fingers. This is an Asian heirloom, purple in color and ready for harvest in 65 days. I slice them down the middle and stir fry them with garlic, adding balsamic vinegar at the end. It makes a great snack, a good choice for growing in containers and a good choice for northern climates.

Diamond eggplant is a slender eggplant originally from Ukraine. It is ready to harvest in 70 days, the fruit is purple ready to harvest when 6 to 9 inches long. This plant remains fairly short around 2 feet tall. Another good choice for northern climates.

Pingtung Long eggplant is a gorgeous lavender color from Taiwan. It is ready to harvest in 70 days, reaching 18 inches in length with a 2 inch diameter. This one for me was more resistant to flea beetles than other varieties.

Galine eggplant is a hybrid that matures in 65 days. It has dark purple, almost black fruit that is bell shaped and 6 to 7 inches long. This variety is similar in shape to the standard Black Beauty but has more tolerance to cooler shorter growing regions.

Some varieties have thorns on stems and calyxes. What is a calyx? It is the green cap that sits at the stem end of an eggplant. This is a very important part of the vegetable when purchasing.

A calyx needs to be a healthy fresh green color. This is how you know that an eggplant has not been sitting on the grocers' shelf too long. Also look for smooth shiny skin for freshness.

Having these purple pendants scattered throughout the garden or decorating your deck add color, texture and interest to the eye.

What is exceptional for eggplant is their spongy texture. Air pockets between cells will collapse when eggplant cooks. Resulting in absorption of the medium that eggplant is cooked in such as oil or any sauce. This can have a negative result or a wonderful positive result. Anyone that has fried eggplant knows too well how greedily it absorbs oil. You can end up with an oily mush. But this absorption can capture flavors that it is cooked in such as sauces, herbs, garlic or lemon. There are several methods to skirt the oily mush ending up with a delicious buttery flavorful texture.

Salting sliced eggplant and leaving it to drain for an hour is an option before frying. Broiling, baking or roasting it over a flame will cook it without frying.

Chapter 15: Herbs

Herbs are in my garden for two reasons. The first reason is to have fresh herbs for cooking and the second is to attract beneficial insects, bees, butterflies and birds. When I hear the low hum of bees or see a butterfly silently flitting through or the swoosh of a hummingbird I know I have a healthy garden. All are aiding the pollination process and the beneficial insects are helping control the destructive insects. I don't have a designated area for most herbs. They are found scattered throughout the garden. Plants of parsley, dill, cilantro and basil are randomly found throughout. The good news is basil is the only one of these herbs that I have to germinate and place in the garden, the other three freely reseed themselves and wind and birds help distribute the seeds.

Parsley

Petroselinum crispum is an Old World biennial that is the most widely used herb in North America. It is a member of the Apiaceae family which also includes carrots and that ever present weed Queen Ann's lace. Its region of origin is the eastern Mediterranean area and has been around for about 5000 years. Greeks and Romans used parsley as a herb but also for medicinal purposes.

In medieval gardens, parsley was considered a pottage herb. A pottage is a thick soup or stew made from an assortment of vegetables, grains and herbs. Some meat, if it was available, but for most it was a meatless dish. Cooked in a big pot over a fire, from which it was eaten, and then more ingredients added over a period of days. So the flavor was always changing.

In the first year of its two year cycle cutting the leaves will activate more leaves to develop. It is frost tolerant and if left for its second year it will produce more leaves along with a central stalk that will flower. Then it happily reseeds itself. If you keep seeds, they remain viable for two years. They are medium feeders so not a lot of fertilizing needs to be done. It needs sun but will do well in partial shade and needs to be thinned after germination. I move the small plants every spring to a different location in the garden. Overall it is an easy plant to have and maintain.

During the first year, roots are confusingly similar to those of a white carrot or parsnip.

Flower configuration is an umbel (think umbrella) with dainty yellow green flowers. Seeds take about 2 to three weeks to germinate so they are a bit slow. The myth that seeds have to travel to hell and back 3,4,5 or 6 times in order for them to germinate depends on who is telling the story. Reality is somewhat different.

There are three varieties of parsley, flat which is also called Italian, the tight curly type and one that is grown for its root which is edible. Consensus is that Italian has more flavor than curly. And dried parsley loses most of its flavor so it is used as an accent or a bit of color.

What can parsley do for you in the garden besides supplying fresh parsley as you need it? Its best potential is in the second year when it flowers which attract a host of critters that you want. One is the braconid wasp and it is your friend. It is tiny, you may confuse it with a fly and it does not sting. It preys on garden pests such as aphids, stink bugs, hornworms to name a few. It lays eggs on a host insect and when hatched the immature wasp consumes the host. Adults get their nourishment from the nectar of the parsley flower.

Another is tachinid fly. It is tiny and mostly unseen. It also lays eggs on a host insect and when eggs hatch the immature fly proceeds to eat its host. The garden pests that they attack are gypsy moths, cutworms, squash bugs and more. Adult flies also feed on the nectar of parsley flowers.

Parsley grows well near peas, carrots, corn, peppers, tomatoes and asparagus. And as an added bonus, after producing seeds small birds are invited into the garden to dine on them.

Basil

King of the garden herbs is Ocimum basilicum and the scent of basil in the garden means summer. It contains a mixture of essential oils which is responsible for its sweet fresh fragrance and it adds a rich green to the garden. It is a member of the Lamiaceae or mint family and in most parts of the world is grown as an annual. However in tropical climates it can be grown as a perennial. It is an Old World plant having its origin in SE Asia, possibly India. There are world wide varieties and it has around 5000 years of existence under its belt.

Egyptians used it in the mummification process. It has been given several magical properties around the world from protection to the poor, giving strength during religious fastings to identifying whether a woman was pure or not. Women always seem to be in the equation somewhere.

Seeds take about a week to germinate and it is an easy herb to grow as long as it has sun and rich moist soil. It is intolerant of frost and drought. So wait until the last frost date before planting and keep the soil moist. It may start out slow due to cool soil temperatures but will settle in and thrive throughout the summer.

A common disease that I see on my basil is leaf spot. Dark circular spots appear on the leaves.

This is due to a fungus which gets started from overhead watering or splashing water on the leaves. Watering just the base of the plant will help keep this in check. If you do see leaves with dark spots then snip them off and put in the trash. Do not add it to your compost pile. Another fungus is powdery mildred. It will appear as grayish dust on leaves but also develop large brown patches on leaves. Again, avoid overhead watering, space plants to maximize air circulation.

Infected leaves and/or plants should be pulled and deposited in the trash.

What insects dine on your basil? The usual suspects such as slugs, snails, aphids, flea beetles and even grasshoppers. Large insects that I can see I pick off and the smaller ones I spray with an insecticidal soap. It does seem to be a favorite snack for deer.

To have a continuous supply of basil just keep pinching off the flower clusters that will try to develop at the tip of a stem. Pinching will increase branching and leaf production which is what you want. But if you have more than one basil plant in the garden and more than enough basil leaves, then let one or more plants develop flowers. The bees will love it.

It seems to grow well planted next to just about anything, tomatoes, peppers, beets and carrots. Once the warmth of summer has arrived it is an easy addition to the garden. Seeds remain viable for five years if kept in a cool dark area.

In the kitchen it is used mainly fresh. Cooking basil destroys the flavor. To minimize this, add basil towards the end of the cooking process.

Rosemary

Salvia rosmarinus is an evergreen Old World perennial bush which is native to dry rocky Mediterranean coasts and has been around for about 7000 years. Its Latin name is rosmarinus and is derived from ros and marinus which means dew of the sea. A legend for the name is Mary, mother of Jesus, when fleeing from Egypt she threw her blue cloak over a bush. The bush had white flowers that turned from white to blue and the plant became Rose of Mary.

Greeks wore garlands of rosemary while taking exams to enhance memory and recall. Brides had rosemary in their bouquets or headpiece as a symbol of love. The old saying 'where rosemary flourished, the woman ruled' had some husbands pulling the plant out of the garden to keep his reputation intact. Burning rosemary in homes was thought to keep the plague at bay.

It is another member of the Lamiaceae or mint family. It is happy in soils that drain well and are on the dry side in a sunny location. It can be used in landscaping pruned into formal shapes or small hedges. Plants can reach 4 to 6 feet tall and life span can be up to 30 years. It is deer resistant which is a big plus for my area.

It, too, has been used since antiquity for cooking and medicinal purposes. In medieval gardens it was grown for the cup or to be distilled. It was infused in water or wine and today some still make tea to tackle sore throats or colds. The small needle shaped leaves of rosemary have a strong flavor so use sparingly for cooking. Hanging sprigs of rosemary in a cool dark place will dry it for future uses. The small stems can be used for skewers for small appetizers such as mozzarella cheese with a cherry tomato.

Some destructive insects that will seek out your rosemary are aphids, whiteflies or mealybugs.

All three are sap sucking insects. Which means what? They feed off a sugary substance that is produced in plant foliage. After a period of time the plant begins to look wilted, yellowed or even deformed.

Aphids seem to be attracted to just about everything. They are soft bodied tiny insects that multiply rapidly. One day there are none and the next it seems as if there are hundreds. Their appearance might resemble tiny bumps on soft stems or underside of leaves. Colors can range from dark brown to a yellowish white. After dining on the sugary substance, they excrete another sugary substance which usually attracts ants. So if you have ants going up and down a plant then the problem may not be ants, it could be aphids. Controlling aphid populations can be done by enticing ladybugs, lacewings and hoverflies to your garden. Also just using a stream of water to knock aphids off your plant will work. The stream of water needs to be hard enough to knock the aphids off but not so hard that it would tear leaves or stems from the plants.

White flies are not flies, look similar to tiny, tiny moths, flutter away when disturbed and are related to aphids. They reproduce quickly, sometimes within 16 days from egg to adult. So numbers of whiteflies could become a nuisance within weeks. Controlling remedies are attracting beneficial insects such as ladybugs, tiny parasitic wasps, and lacewings, but also hummingbirds and dragonflies that dine on white flies. Hanging sticky traps or using row covers will help capture or deter them. Insecticidal soaps, neem oil or just blasting your plant with water. The water will knock the whiteflies from their perch robbing them of their source of nourishment.

Mealybugs are soft, oval insects that have a wax covering and filaments that stand up all over their body. They are slow to non moving at different life stages. You usually find them in colonies during warm weather in areas that did not experience cold winters or on indoor plants. Ladybugs, lacewings and spiders all have good appetites for mealybugs. Because of the insect's wax covering most insecticides are not effective. As with the previously mentioned pests a good blasting of water will help keep mealybugs under control.

Rosemary can become a victim of root rot if it is in soil that is constantly moist. Root rot is a generic term for different pathogens that attack root systems. There are usually no visible signs of the disease until it is too late. Plants will be wilted but the soil is moist. Examining the roots will show soft brown roots which may stink. If you suspect that your plant is a victim of root rot, then you need to throw the plant away and discard the soil. Do not use the soil again because the pathogen that caused the problem is still in the soil. Don't over water plants!

The flowers of rosemary will attract a host of beneficial insects from bees to butterflies. Once rosemary is established it is drought tolerant and a low maintenance plant. Check your planting zone to determine if rosemary should be protected during winter.

Dill

Dill is an Old World annual that adds grace and interest in a vegetable garden. It is another member of the Apiaceae family along with parsley and carrots. Its place of origin is thought to be in the Mediterranean region. First recorded history is usage as a medicinal herb by ancient Egyptians 5000 years ago. It was still used as a medicinal or infirmary herb in the Middle Ages because of its ability to lull or quiet the sick. Dill was also hung on doorways to ward off witches. It was an ingredient in ancient Greek wines. Seeds were chewed for a breath freshener and to quiet children during long religious services. The word dill comes to us from old Norse 'dylla' which meant to sooth or lull.

Some varieties reach heights of 2 to 3 feet that are willowy swaying in a breeze. Stalks are hollow and can bend or break in strong winds. These stalks end with a cluster of tiny yellow flowers that have a shape that reminds you of an umbrella. There are dwarf varieties that only reach a height of 2 feet or less. Leaves on dwarf dill tend to be more abundant. These are suitable for container gardening. The leaves are referred to as dill weed and are very thin and feathery. Fresh dill weed has a burst of flavor which is much stronger than dry dill weed. If your main goal is dill weed and not the seeds then try a dwarf variety because these plants produce more leaves than the tall varieties.

If seeds are not harvested, they fall to the ground and freely germinate, supplying you with a continuous yearly crop of dill to the point of becoming a nuisance. Dill marries well with salmon, peas, lemons, any combination of fresh salads, potatoes, an essential component of tzatziki and eggs. And, of course, pickled cucumbers. The list is almost endless.

Dill does best in cool weather. Temperatures that go above 80 F initiates seed production. It does best in a sunny location in soil that has good drainage. It is considered a light feeder even growing in poor soils. After being established it is somewhat drought tolerant. It is a low maintenance plant.

It is a wonderful host plant for butterflies and bees when flowering. Also ladybugs, lacewings, aphid midges, braconid wasps and hoverflies are attracted to dill. These insects are the good guys and in turn devour pests such as aphids.

Ladybug is the Americanized name for Ladybird which has been used in England for hundreds of years. It is a species of beetle, adults can fly and some species have bright color combinations on their oval bodies. The most common color combination for home gardeners is red/orange with black dots. This beneficial insect will consume aphids.

Lacewings are about ¾ of an inch long, green in color and have lacy delicate wings. After a lacewing egg has hatched, the larvae or juvenile lacewing eat soft bodied insects such as aphids and some caterpillars. They have voracious appetites as any teenager. Adult lacewings prefer to dine on nectar and keep laying more eggs.

Aphid midges are tiny delicate flies. Adults feed on the sugary substance or honeydew that aphids produce and then lay eggs near the aphids. When the larvae hatch they will attach themselves to an aphid, paralyzing the aphid and then eating it at their leisure.

A hoverfly can be confused with a bee or wasp. But it does not have a stinger and it only has one set of wings. Bees and wasps have two sets of wings. Adult hoverflies dine on nectar from flowers, lay eggs, and then, it is the larvae that attack soft bodied insects for nourishment such as aphids or caterpillars. They get their name because they have the ability to hover over flowers selecting their nectar before darting to the next flower.

Dill in my garden germinates freely in random places and grows next to everything.

Cilantro or Coriander?

One more Old World native is coriander. In most of the world the whole plant is coriander. However Spanish speaking countries refer to the leaves and stem of coriander as cilantro. In North America the word cilantro has been adopted to refer to the leaves and stem. Mature dried seeds have kept the name coriander.

Its area of origin is from southern Europe, northern Africa to western Asia. It is an annual that is loved or hated because of its taste. Those that cannot tolerate cilantro have a gene that is responsible for detecting aldehyde chemicals. This chemical has a soapy taste. It may be one of the oldest herbs possibly going back as far as 6000 years. Seeds have been found in ancient caves in Israel and King Tut's tomb in Egypt. It is also known as Chinese parsley and Mexican parsley.

Another member of the Apiaceae family, it has thin stalks that reach 2 feet high with feathery leaves which resemble flat leaved parsley. Leaves are fragile, do not have a long storage life and are used mostly fresh. Cooking cilantro diminishes its flavor so use it fresh and add as a last garnish.

It is easy to grow in sun or partial shade. Heat of summer will make it bolt. If left to go to seed then the seeds can be harvested. Seeds are round and seed color will change from green to brown. So you can end up with cilantro, an herb and coriander seeds, a spice from one plant. If seeds are not harvested then it reseeds itself happily year after year.

Planted near any leafy vegetables such as the cabbage family, spinach or lettuce it will attract beneficial insects such as ladybugs and lacewings which in turn prey on pests such as aphids and spider mites. Planting cilantro with dill will create a magnet for beneficial insects.

Thyme

Another member of the Lamiaceae or mint family is thyme. Its region of origin is the Mediterranean/Eurasia area. It is a perennial evergreen low growing shrub that can have a lifespan of 5 to 6 years. In ancient times it was regarded as an herb that would give you courage.

Thymus vulgaris is the common garden variety. Leaves can be used both fresh or dried and the flowers are edible also. This is another herb that has been around for thousands of years for culinary purposes. It is a major ingredient in Arab's za'atar, French bouquet garni and herbs de Provence. It was one of many herbs used by the Egyptians for embalming.

A sunny location with well drained soil is needed. Once established this herb is drought tolerant. If left in constantly moist soil, root rot could develop. It requires minimal fertilizing so overall this herb is an easy low maintenance plant to have. Flowers are typically lavender in color and the whole mound of thyme could be encased in beautiful lavender flowers. And when it flowers the bees are very active.

Oregano

Yet one more member of the Lamiaceae or mint family is oregano. A perennial shrub in temperate climates but in colder climates it is treated as an annual. It has its place of origin in the Mediterranean region. Along with rosemary and thyme, this herb does well in warm dry conditions. The name comes down through several languages but has its source from Greek.

Meaning 'mountain brightness or joy'. Myth being that this herb was created by Aphrodite for her garden.

Chewing the leaves was believed to alleviate such maladies as stomach aches, fever, and toothaches to name a few. Its reputation was an all encompassing answer to just about everything. Elizabethan England cherished it for its ability to promote happiness and tranquility. It was an answer to all of life's problems. Americans were late to enjoy oregano. GIs returning from the second WW came home with a craving for pizza and of course in Italy oregano was one of the components of pizza.

Full sun and well drained soil are a must for oregano. It doesn't need rich soil so if you have an area that is unproductive for most plants then oregano will fill that slot. It will start out as a low growing mound but grow to reach 2 feet tall. Flowers will develop on stalks and range in color from white to pink to purple. It is drought tolerant once established but could develop root rot if left in moist soil that does not drain well.

A beneficial insect that will visit is the hoverfly sometimes referred to as flower fly that will devour aphids. Why the two names? These insects hover over flowers dining on the nectar and pollen. They look similar to bees or wasps but do not sting. So their disguise as a bee or wasp makes predators leave them alone. They visit a long list of flowers helping to keep your garden healthy. Oregano is one more low maintenance plant to have in your garden.

Chapter 16: Recipes

Growing up we ate a lot of cabbage. Stuffed cabbage leaves, sauerkraut, different cabbage salads and fried cabbage. In Oklahoma we fried everything. All we needed was a cast iron skillet and oil. Not healthy, but oh so addictive. Here is my version of fried cabbage.

Fried Cabbage

Heat 2 Tablespoons peanut oil in a skillet, when hot add 2 Tablespoons sesame seeds and 1 teaspoon of red pepper flakes stirring constantly. When sesame seeds are heated they will start to pop. At this point I add ½ yellow onion that has been sliced into half moon shapes, ¼ inch thick. Cook onions until clear then add 4 cups of sliced ½ inch wide cabbage. Don't worry if it looks as if it won't fit. Keep stirring and the cabbage will cook down. I stir fry until cabbage has reduced its volume and there is still some crispness to the cabbage. If you like soft cabbage then just fry a little longer. Add salt to taste. Serves two.

Red Cabbage Slaw

Thinly slice 4 cups red cabbage; peel, core and grate 1 apple; peel and grate 1 carrot and mix together with ½ cup golden raisins in a bowl. Add 4 Tablespoons extra virgin olive oil and 2 Tablespoons rice vinegar to mixture tossing to incorporate. Taste and add juice of 1 lemon as needed to bring up the flavors. I don't use any salt for this recipe. Chill for several hours. Serves two.

Krumb Makmur or Stewed Cabbage

This is an Egyptian recipe. Easy and delicious.

Slice cabbage ½ inch thick and 2 inches long. Slice enough for 4 cups. Place cabbage in a pot, add enough water to cover, add 1 teaspoon ground coriander and parboil for 3 to 5 minutes.

Drain water. Add 1 cup tomato sauce to cabbage and cook for 15 to 20 minutes on low heat. Stir occasionally. Salt to taste. Serves 2.

Cabbage Salad

Thinly slice enough cabbage for 4 cups. Place in a bowl with 2 Tablespoons extra virgin olive oil and juice of ½ a lemon or more. Toss. Salt to taste just before serving. Salting it beforehand releases water from the cabbage and then you have a limp salad, not a crunchy one. This is an excellent dish to accompany fish. Serves two.

Easy Brussel Sprouts

Take ½ pound Brussel sprouts removing outer leaves if damaged or yellow. Slice in half lengthwise and steam until a skewer can pierce but with some resistance. You don't want them cooked completely at this point. Melt 2 to 3 Tablespoons of unsalted butter in a saucepan with a pinch of sugar. Add the steamed Brussel sprouts and saute for several minutes. Serves two.

Easy Brussel Sprouts # 2

Trim ½ pound Brussel sprouts and slice in half lengthwise. Drizzle some olive oil and 2 Tablespoons unsalted butter in a non-stick skillet. Heat to melt butter and mix with olive oil. Place Brussel sprouts cut side down in one layer in the skillet, sprinkle with salt and pepper. Cover and cook over low heat until Brussel sprouts are tender. Do not flip the sprouts. After about 5 to 7 minutes the cut side will be browned. Serve immediately. Serves two.

Easy Brussel Sprouts # 3

Sometimes I will caramelize a handful of nuts in brown sugar or maple syrup to add to cooked Brussel sprouts. It just gives a little sweetness to the sprouts.

Broccoli Cheese soup.

This is my favorite soup.

Melt 3 Tablespoons unsalted butter in a soup pot then add 1 cup chopped yellow onion and ⅛ teaspoon nutmeg. Cook until the onion is soft and translucent. This should take about 3 to 5 minutes. Add 1 Tablespoon minced garlic and cook just a few seconds until fragrant. Add salt, pepper and 3 Tablespoons of unbleached flour, stirring until blended. Cook for at least 2 minutes to remove the flour taste. Add 3 cups vegetable stock slowly whisking to incorporate. Bring to a boil, reduce heat and simmer until liquid thickens. Add 1 pound of broccoli with stems peeled if tough and cut into small pieces. Cook until broccoli is tender 5 to 6 minutes. Remove from heat and blend mixture. I don't blend until smooth because I like having small random pieces of broccoli in the soup. I use a hand held blender for this. Now add ½ cup heavy cream, heat until it simmers and then add 1 ¼ cups shredded Cheddar cheese. Stir until melted. Adjust salt to taste. It is fast, easy and a winter satisfying soup.

Simple simple broccoli.

One medium size broccoli head. Cut florets off into serving sizes. Slice peeled stem in 1 inch thick pieces. Blanch in boiling salted water for about 3 minutes. Drain. Add 3 Tablespoons of unsalted butter to broccoli, a pinch of salt and saute in the melted butter for several minutes.

Stirring the broccoli frequently. Cook until you have the consistency that you want. Soft or al dente. Serves two.

Simple simple broccoli #2

One medium size broccoli head. Cut florets off into serving sizes. Slice peeled stem in 1 inch thick pieces. Peel and slice 4 garlic cloves. Saute garlic in 2 Tablespoons of olive oil until the garlic starts to sizzle. Place broccoli in the pan. Stir until a deep green color is obtained. Pour ¼ cup chicken broth and cover, cooking for 5 to 10 minutes until done to your liking. Serves two.

Cauliflower salad.

Cut cauliflower into florets. Steam for ten minutes. Cauliflower should be easily pierced but with some resistance. Don't cook it until it is soft. Place in a salad bowl and let cool. Mix ¼ cup olive oil and juice of one lemon stirring to emulsify. Pour over cauliflower. Salt and pepper to taste. This is a good salad to serve with fish. Serve at room temperature for two.

Fried Cauliflower.

Cut cauliflower into serving pieces. Steam for about 5 minutes, let cool. Heat one inch canola oil in a frying pan then add cauliflower. Fry until cauliflower starts to brown, turning frequently.

Drain on paper towels, salt to taste and sprinkle with cumin. Serve warm or at room temperature. Will make two servings.

Fried Cauliflower #2 Another Variation.

Trim leaves from cauliflower. Place the whole head in a large saucepan with 1 inch of water. Cover and braise until cauliflower can be pierced but with some resistance. Drain and remove. Cool and cut into serving pieces. Deep fry pieces in canola oil until portions start to brown.

Drain on paper towels and salt. Serve warm. Make two servings.

Easy Pepper Salad

Broil 4 or 5 bell peppers until skins are blistered. Turn peppers frequently to avoid scorching. You want to end up with a soft pepper with skins that just peel away leaving just meat. You can use all green or mix it up with different colors of bell peppers. Sometimes we mix sweet and hot chilis together to give a little extra pop to the salad. Once peppers are cooled then peel and remove seeds. Cut into strips and place in a serving bowl. Mince 3 garlic cloves, 2 to 3 Tablespoons of olive oil and 2 Tablespoons of red vinegar. Mix and salt to taste.

Chili Rellenos

Broil 4 Poblano chilis until skin blisters and chili is soft. Do not burn the skin or you will have very little if any meat left. Cool, peel, pull stems out and remove seeds. Using Queso de Oaxaca or Monterey Jack cheese cut 8 sticks of cheese about ¼ inch square and 3 inches long. Put two cheese sticks in the cavity of each chili. Don't worry if the chilis split. The batter will seal everything.

To make the batter, separate 3 eggs. Beat egg whites until stiff peaks form. Whisk egg yolks with 3 Tablespoons flour, a pinch of salt and 1 Tablespoon water. Fold stiff egg whites into yolk mixture. Heat ½ cup oil in a frying pan. Take a stuffed chili and place it in the batter, coating it on all sides. Again don't worry if the batter isn't even. It will all work out. Using your hands place battered chili in hot oil. I fry two at a time. Frying doesn't take long, maybe 1 minute or so on each side. Fry until the batter is golden brown. Gently turn over and brown. Cheese melts quickly and is creamy. Remove to a plate that has a paper towel on it. Repeat process for remaining chilis. Serve warm. Serves two. Enjoy.

Green Tomato Mincemeat Cookies

To make green tomato mincemeat, you will need 2 cups of finely chopped green tomatoes. Discard the juice. You will also need 2 cups chopped tart apples, ¼ cup white vinegar, 1 lb. raisins, 2 cups of sugar, 1 teaspoon each of salt, allspice, cloves and cinnamon. Mix all together and cook until thick. Stir frequently. Cool mixture. Place 1 ½ cups of mincemeat in small freezer bags and freeze. The mincemeat will not freeze solid.

To make the cookie dough, cream 1 cup unsalted butter and 1 ½ cups of sugar until fluffy. Then add 3 beaten eggs, 1 ½ cups thawed green tomato mincemeat, 3 ½ cups unbleached flour, ½ teaspoon salt and 1 teaspoon soda. Add 1 cup chopped nuts if desired. Spoon 1 to 2 Tablespoons of dough, depending on size of desired cookie, on a greased cookie sheet or a cookie sheet lined with parchment paper. Bake in a 400 degree oven for 12 to 15 minutes.

Cream of tomato soup.

Simmer 2 ½ cups peeled chopped fresh tomatoes, ½ cup chopped celery, ¼ cup chopped onion and 1 teaspoon sugar for 15 minutes. The tomatoes will release water as they cook but stir occasionally and watch for scotching. Remove from heat and let mixture cool. Then I use a handheld immersion blender to puree. Strain this mixture using a spoon and hand held strainer. Push the liquid through the strainer until the remaining pulp is somewhat dry. Discard the dry pulp.

Reheat and slowly add 2 cups vegetable or chicken broth. Next prepare 2 cups of béchamel sauce and slowly whisk this into the mixture. Adjust seasoning if necessary.

Sometimes I add 1 teaspoon of tomato paste at the end to boost tomato flavor if needed. Bring back up to a simmer. Ladle into bowls and enjoy. Two to three servings.

Bechamel Sauce.

Melt 2 Tablespoons of unsalted butter in a saucepan then add 2 Tablespoons of flour. Whisk flour mixture to eliminate clumps cooking over low heat for 2 to 3 minutes. Slowly add 2 cups of milk whisking constantly to incorporate into the flour mixture. Bring to a gentle simmer, whisking constantly and cook until mixture thickens and is smooth. If the mixture coats the back of a spoon then it is thick enough.

Ralph's Tomato Sauce.

In a saucepan add 1 Tablespoon of olive oil and fry ½ small chopped onion. Fry until the onion is translucent. Add two cloves of garlic coarsely chopped and fry for one to two minutes. In the meantime cut 2 pounds peeled* plum tomatoes into small pieces (or you can use one 28 ounce can of San Marzano tomatoes, but you will need to crush them) adding to onions. Add 2 or 3 whole fresh basil leaves. Cover and simmer on low heat for 30 to 45 minutes. Mash mixture with potato masher as the mixture cooks. Salt and pepper to taste. Can be used immediately or let cool and freeze. Great to have this on hand.

*Place fresh tomatoes in boiling water for about 1 minute. Skin will start to crack. Remove from water, cool to handle and skin can be pulled off easily.

It seems every cuisine around the Mediterranean has a version of potato salad. This is mine. I don't boil potatoes but bake them retaining more potato flavor. I use russets for this dish.

Calico Potato Salad

Combine 2 large or 3 medium Russet potatoes that have been baked, cooled, peeled and chopped, 1 peeled and shredded carrot, 1 thinly sliced stalk of celery, ½ diced red bell pepper and ½ cup chopped red onion. Mix together ½ cup of mayonnaise, ½ cup sour cream, 2 Tablespoons rice vinegar, 1 teaspoon Dijon mustard and salt and pepper to taste. Add this dressing to the potato/vegetable mixture. Dressing should just hold the potato mixture together. There is nothing worse than a potato salad that is swimming in dressing to the point that you cannot taste potato. Chill and adjust salt and pepper if needed. Serves three or four.

Perunasalaatti, Finnish Potato Salad

Boil three red or Yukon Gold potatoes until a skewer inserted pierces the potato easily, peel and dice them when cool. Mix potatoes, ½ peeled and diced apple, ¼ cup diced dill pickle and ¼ cup diced red onion. Whip ½ cup heavy cream until stiff peaks form. Combine ⅓ cup mayonnaise, ⅓ cup sour cream, 1 Tablespoon Dijon mustard, ½ teaspoon tarragon, 1 Tablespoon white wine vinegar and salt and pepper to taste. Fold dressing into whipped cream. Add the dressing to the potato mixture. Adjust salt and pepper if necessary and chill until ready to serve. Three to four servings.

Middle Eastern Potato Salad

This is so easy, quick and delicious.

Boil ½ pound small white potatoes. Yukon Gold is good for this. Cook until a skewer slides through the potato easily. Cool and slice thin. Mix ¼ cup of fresh lemon juice and ¼ cup of olive oil. Blend the two with a fork until it is emulsified. Arrange potato slices on a serving plate and pour lemon juice/olive oil mixture over potatoes. They will absorb lemon oil mixture. Slice two green onions and chop ¼ cup of parsley. Sprinkle garlic salt or seasoned salt over potatoes and garnish with the green onions and parsley. Serves three or four.

Layered Potato Dish

Boil 1 pound potatoes in their skins or jackets until the skewer pierces easily. Drain and peel when cool. Slice them ¼ inch wide. Set aside. Cook 1 to 2 slices of smoked bacon until crispy. Remove, cool and crumble. Set aside. Butter a baking dish that will hold the sliced potatoes in 1 layer. Sprinkle 2 Tablespoons of bread crumbs over the bottom of the buttered dish. Arrange sliced potatoes in the dish.

In a medium skillet, melt 4 Tablespoons unsalted butter over low heat and add ⅓ pound of grated Kashkaval cheese. Stir until smooth and bubbling. Add the crumbled bacon, 2 Tablespoons of bread crumbs, 1 Tablespoon dry dill, salt and pepper to taste. Stir mixture until creamy. Pour the contents evenly over potatoes. You have to work fast to get it even. Bake for 20 minutes at 350F. Serve at once! Two to three servings. Just a note that if you did not get the cheese mixture spread evenly then all is not lost. Bake anyway and it is still delicious.

Some Smashed Potatoes

Boil 4 to 5 golf ball size unpeeled potatoes in salted water until a skewer can easily pierce through. Drain, do not peel. Add 3 Tablespoons unsalted butter, 3 to 4 Tablespoons sour cream, salt and pepper to taste. Use a fork or potato masher to smash the mixture. You will have lumps and you want lumps. If the mixture is too thick, incorporate a small amount of half and half. If you have chives then chop some and add to the mixture. Serves two.

Carrot Ginger Soup

Combine 1 Tablespoon unsalted butter and 1 chopped yellow onion in a large saucepan. Cook until onions are translucent, stirring often. Add 3 cups chicken broth, 5 cups of scraped or peeled and sliced carrots and 1 ½ Tablespoon grated fresh ginger. Cover, bring to a boil. Reduce heat and simmer until carrots are tender. This doesn't take long, just several minutes. Remove from heat. Puree the carrot mixture. I use a hand held Immersion blender. Blend until smooth. Add ½ cup half and half and heat again. Do not let it boil. Add salt and pepper to taste. Ladle into bowls and top with a dollop of sour cream. Wonderful on a winter's day. Serves two to three.

Glazed Carrots.

Scrape or peel and slice 2 carrots. Place carrots in a saucepan with 2 Tablespoons of unsalted butter, 3 Tablespoons of brown sugar and pepper. Stir until the butter and brown sugar have melted. Cover and simmer for several minutes until the carrots are glazed. Stir frequently.

If using fresh carrots out of the garden there is no need to peel just scrape the carrots with a paring knife. A finishing touch to glazed carrots add 1 Tablespoon chopped parsley and 1 Tablespoon minced garlic to the carrots just before serving. Serves two.

Carrot Salad

Scrape or peel and shred 2 carrots. Thinly slice 1 cup of purple cabbage. Mix the two. Color combinations should be carrots are prominent but the purple cabbage adds enough of a distraction for interest. Add 1 cup walnuts and ½ cup dried cranberries. Mix together and add 2 Tablespoons of a good creamy poppy seed dressing. Mix again and let it sit for an hour. Serves two.

Carrot Sticks

Scrape or peel 2 carrots. Slice into 2 inch sticks. Squeeze the juice of 1 lime over carrots sticks. It is amazing how the lime juice brings up the carrot flavor. A quick and easy appetizer.

Sprinkle salt if you must. Serves two to three.

Beet Salad

I bake beets instead of boiling them. Cut leaves off but leave an inch of stem attached to the root. Wash 4 or 5 beets, put them in a baking pan, cover with foil (no water). I use a bread pan for this and bake at 400 degrees for about 45 minutes or until a skewer pierces them easily. After the beets are cool you should be able to just rub the skin off. Slice off the top stem pieces and a small portion of root. Slice beets 1/4 inch thick. Add one or two minced garlic cloves, 2 to 3 Tablespoons olive oil and 1 to 2 Tablespoons red wine vinegar. Mix and taste. Adjust oil and vinegar to taste if needed. This salad will keep for several days. Serves two to three.

Beet and Kale Salad

Bake 1 or 2 beets. Put them in a baking pan, cover with foil (no water)and bake 400 F for 45 or until a skewer pierces them easily. Cool and rub skin to remove it. Slice off the top stem pieces and a small portion of root. Wash and dry 6 or 7 kale leaves. Cut kale down on both sides of the kale rib to remove the rib. Compost kale rib. Chop kale leaf pieces until the size of a dime. Put in a bowl, sprinkle with ¾ teaspoon of salt and massage kale for 2 minutes. This works the salt in but also softens the kale leaf. Dry pan roast 1 cup pecans until fragrant. Just a couple of minutes stirring while roasting. Add 5 Tablespoons of maple syrup to the pecan pan and stir.

This will glaze the pecans. Remove from heat and cool until you can handle pecans to break them into small pieces. Cut cooked beets into bite size pieces and add to kale. Add glazed pecans. Make a vinaigrette with 2 Tablespoons balsamic vinegar, 1 Tablespoon fresh lemon juice and ¼ cup of olive oil. Whisk together until emulsified and pour over salad. Serve immediately. Note: use real maple syrup. Serves two to three.

Tzatziki is a wonderful Greek salad made from yogurt and cucumbers.

Combine 2 cups plain yogurt, 1 medium cucumber that has been peeled, diced small and seeds removed if large, 2 minced garlic cloves, 2 to 3 Tablespoons olive oil, 1 Tablespoon white vinegar, 1 Tablespoon chopped fresh dill, 1 teaspoon chopped fresh mint and a pinch of salt.

Mix all ingredients and chill. Wonderful as a salad but also a dip or topping on fried eggplant or fried zucchini. Serves three to four.

Cucumbers in oil and lemon juice

This is such a simple simple recipe.

Peel and slice enough cucumbers for 2 to 3 cups. Place in a serving bowl, add 3 Tablespoons of olive oil and juice of half a lemon or juice of one lime. Add a pinch of salt but only just before serving. Salt will draw water out of the cucumbers and they will be limp. There is nothing worse than a limp cucumber. It is ready to be served. Great served with seafood. Serves two.

Cool and Creamy Cucumber Salad

Peel 2 cucumbers that are about 7 inches long, cut into thin, thin slices and place them in a large bowl. Sprinkle cucumbers with ½ teaspoon salt, 1 Tablespoon lemon juice and ¼ teaspoon sugar. Gently toss. Let stand for 30 minutes. Drain, gently pressing out liquid with the back of a spoon. Pat dry. In a medium bowl whisk 1 cup sour cream until light. Add 1 small minced shallot, 2 Tablespoons cider vinegar, ¾ teaspoon sugar, ½ teaspoon celery seed, 1 Tablespoon chopped chives, salt and pepper to sour cream. Place one layer of cucumber slices in a shallow serving bowl. Spoon one third sour cream mixture over the top. Then sprinkle chopped fresh dill. Total amount of chopped dill should be around ¼ cup. Repeat until all ingredients are used. Sprinkle top with pepper to taste. Chill. Serves fours.

A very fast and easy green bean salad recipe.

Steam ½ pound green beans until they are the texture or al dente that you prefer. Let them cool. Place them in a bowl. Mince 3 cloves of garlic and add to beans. Mix in 3 Tablespoons of extra virgin olive oil. Add juice of one lemon. Salt to taste. Enjoy! Serves two.

An easy and delicious green bean dish.

Steam ½ pound green beans until they are the texture or al dente that you prefer. Heat 1 Tablespoon of extra virgin olive oil in a skillet. Add ¼ cup sliced almonds, fry slightly, don't brown. Add the steamed green beans with ¼ cup of sun dried tomatoes. Salt if needed. Saute until heated. Serves two.

Bean Salad

Soak 1 cup of dried Jacob's Cattle beans or any dry white bean overnight. Drain and cook in boiling salted water for ½ an hour until al dente. Keep tasting, don't overcook. Drain and cool. Place beans in a bowl with ¼ minced yellow onion, ¼ cup chopped Italian parsley, juice of 1 lemon and 2 Tablespoons of extra virgin olive oil. Mix and salt to taste. Serve at room temperature. Serves two.

Bean and Cabbage Soup

This soup I make with a slice of smoked ham.

Rinse ⅔ cup of dried white beans and add to 4 cups vegetable broth. Cook for ½ hour or until the beans are almost al dente. Chop 4 cups of cabbage into bite size pieces and add to broth. Dice the ham slice and add to cabbage along with 1 teaspoon salt, 1 teaspoon dried thyme and 1 cup of water. Simmer for 1 hour, taste for salt and add more water if the soup is too thick. It is a delicious winter soup made with winter cabbage and summer dried beans from the garden. This is one of those soups that is good on the first day and great on the second day! Three to four servings.

Easy Peas

Put ¾ cup of water and a pinch of salt in a small saucepan. Bring to a boil then add 1 ½ cups of fresh or frozen peas. Bring back to a boil cooking until the peas are tender. Several minutes depending on whether using fresh or frozen. Drain water, add 2 Tablespoons of unsalted butter and a pinch of salt. Saute peas in the butter for 2 minutes and serve hot. Serves two.

There are so many variations of the three following pea recipes but I want to taste the peas so I keep it simple.

Peas a la Francaise

Melt 2 Tablespoons of unsalted butter and add 24 small pearl onions that have been peeled and sliced in half. Cook over low heat until onions are translucent and beginning to come apart. This may take 3 or 4 minutes. Now add 1 small head of Boston lettuce that has been cut into 2 inch pieces with 1 ½ pounds fresh peas or 2 ½ cups frozen peas. Add a pinch of salt if you wish, cover and cook over low heat for another 5 minutes or so. Taste a pea and if it is tender then it is ready. Bring to the table hot! Serves four. Cooked lettuce adds a nice spring flavor to anything. This dish goes well with pork chops.

Peas Roman Style

Melt ¼ cup of unsalted butter in a saucepan and add 1 small diced onion. Cook until onions are slightly brown. Add 2 cups fresh or frozen peas, 2 Tablespoons of water, salt and pepper cooking until peas are tender. Stir frequently. Add 5 slices of shredded prosciutto, mix and heat throughout. Serves four.

English Peas With Mint.

Saute 1 sliced green onion in 2 Tablespoons of olive oil just until the onion is tender. Add 2 cups fresh or frozen peas, a pinch of salt and enough water to cover peas. Bring to a boil and cook for 2 minutes. Add 5 chopped mint leaves. To chop the mint, first remove the main rib and then chop the remaining leaf. Continue cooking until peas are tender. About 2 more minutes. Adjust seasoning and serve warm. Serves four.

Hamburger, peas and rice. This recipe is from my mother-in-law and it was very kid friendly in our house.

Mince 1 large onion and fry in 2 Tablespoons unsalted butter until very light brown. Add ¾ pound lean ground beef and cook until the beef is no longer pink. As the beef is cooking, smash it with the back of a large spoon until it has crumbled. Salt and pepper to taste.

Rinse 1 cup of short grain rice to remove some of the starch. The water will look milky. Cook rice according to directions on the package.

In a separate saucepan bring 1 ½ cups of water and a pinch of salt to boil. Add 1 cup of fresh or frozen peas. When it returns to a boil then let them tumble around in the boiling water for several minutes or until tender. Drain.

You now have three pans containing the meat-onion mixture, rice and peas.

Place a couple of large spoonfuls of rice on an individual plate, then add one or two spoonfuls of meat mixture and finally top off with a spoonful of drained peas. You now have a mound on the plate to mix around and the flavors complement each other. It is a fast and easy meal.

The best way to eat a pea is straight out of the garden. Peas are 25% sugar by weight and sugar changes to starch rapidly if not refrigerated. Recipes for peas should never be complicated or lengthy as either would obliterate the tender taste of a pea.

Wilted lettuce.

This is a classic Southern salad.

Place 8 cups of torn leaf lettuce in a bowl. Fry 3 strips of bacon until crisp, remove from the pan and blot excessive bacon grease from the meat. Keep 2 or 3 Tablespoons of bacon drippings which could be the whole amount in the pan. While still hot add 2 to 3 Tablespoons of apple cider vinegar, stir to mix the two. It will sizzle. Immediately pour over lettuce, add 2 or 3 chopped green onions and the crumbled bacon. Mix and salt to taste. Enjoy. Serves two.

Vinegar Spinach.

Wash spinach well. I dunk it in a sink full of cold water, remove, drain water and do it all over again to remove any soil particles. Place wet spinach in a large saucepan without additional water, cover and place over low heat. It will steam and wilt. This will only take a few minutes. Keep checking it to avoid scorching. Drain, place in a bowl and sprinkle 1 to 2 Tablespoons of apple cider vinegar over spinach and serve immediately while warm. This was our standard spinach dish growing up. Serves two.

Creamed Spinach.

Steam 10 oz. of spinach as in the recipe above. Drain squeezing liquid out and then chop. Melt 1 Tablespoon of unsalted butter in a medium frying pan adding spinach, ¼ teaspoon of nutmeg and ½ cup of cream. Cook over low heat, stirring constantly until cream is incorporated into spinach. Bring to the table warm. Serves two.

Strawberry Spinach Salad

To make a dressing for this salad, combine 3 Tablespoons of sugar, ⅛ teaspoon of paprika, ½ teaspoon of prepared mustard, ¼ cup canola oil, ¼ cup apple cider vinegar and 1 ½ teaspoon minced onion. Blend with a fork until emulsified or blended. Now put a handful of washed clean dry spinach in a bowl, add four sliced strawberries to spinach and spoon some dressing over the spinach mixture. Toss to coat evenly. So you can make an individual salad or a larger version for your family. Dressing will keep several days refrigerated. Adding toasted walnuts is an added bonus.

This is a version of a Greek eggplant salad. It is simply wonderful.

Melitzanosalata

Cook ¾ pound eggplant. This can be done several ways. Cook unpeeled eggplant over a gas flame until the skin is crisp and darkened, turning it occasionally. Or cook unpeeled eggplant under a broiler until the skin is crisp and darkened, turning it occasionally. Or peel eggplant, cube it and fry in 2 Tablespoons olive oil. If using this third method then oil needs to be very hot to reduce the amount of oil that eggplant will absorb. Stir fry until eggplant is soft, reducing the amount of olive oil in the dressing.

Let the eggplant cool. Remove charred skin if eggplant has been cooked in one of the first two methods and chop eggplant pulp. Place eggplant in a bowl along with 1 large chopped tomato, 1 green pepper that has been seeded and finely chopped, 1 medium chopped onion and 2 cloves crushed garlic. Dressing for this salad is 3 Tablespoons of red wine vinegar, ¼ cup of olive oil, salt and pepper to taste. Whisk together and pour over vegetables. Toss and chill. Sprinkle some chopped fresh parsley before serving. Serves two to four.

Fried Eggplant

Peel and slice 1 eggplant. Slices should be at least 1/4 inch thick. Make an egg wash with 1 beaten egg along with 1 Tablespoon of water. Dip slices of eggplant in egg mixture and then coat eggplant with your favorite bread crumbs. I use Italian style bread crumbs. Heat 1/8 inch of oil in a skillet. I use canola oil. When oil is hot, place several slices in a skillet frying on both sides. Eggplant does not absorb oil when frying because the beaten egg serves as a barrier.

Frying on both sides just takes a minute or two. Fry until it is crispy turning brown. To finish you have two choices. Dust the fried eggplant with garlic powder and salt. Or take 1 cup of sour cream and add 2 cloves of minced fresh garlic. If you take the sour cream route then mix this letting it sit for several hours to acquire a garlic flavor. Put a dollop of sour cream mixture on a slice of eggplant and enjoy! And as a bonus you have now become an honorary Okie.

Marinated Fried Eggplant

An Arab dish eaten at room temperature.

Peel 1 eggplant and cut crosswise into 1/2 inch slices. In a heavy skillet over medium high heat add ½ cup of canola oil until hot. Fry several slices of eggplant for a few minutes. As it sizzles, flip and continue frying on the other side. Cook until golden brown. Do not overcook. Continue until all the eggplant has been fried. Eggplant will absorb a lot of oil. You may have to add more oil as you continue to fry. When cooked, place on paper towels and let rest for a couple of hours. (I place newspapers on the bottom and then paper towel sheets). There will be a lot of oil released.

Pour off oil remaining in the skillet, reserving about 2 tablespoons. Reduce heat and add 6 cloves of sliced garlic, cook until it sizzles. Do not overcook, this will take 1 or 2 minutes. Turn off and remove from heat. After the eggplant has rested and released some oil then place three eggplant slices in a shallow bowl and spread a few slices of garlic. Sprinkle a little vinegar and salt.

Repeat until all eggplant is used. Add more vinegar and salt if you wish. Serves two to three.

Babaghannoush

Cook a whole unpeeled eggplant. There are several ways to do this. If you have a gas stove then you can lay eggplant on top of a burner at the lowest setting slowly roasting the eggplant, turning it several times until the skin is black and eggplant is soft. This gives the eggplant a charcoal flavor that is absent from other methods of cooking. It can be cooked under a broiler or baked, again turning it several times until the skin is black and eggplant is soft. If using this method then lay eggplant on a cookie sheet to catch any juices from falling in the oven.

When the cooked eggplant is cool enough to handle, peel it. Put the pulp in a bowl mashing it with a fork. Add 2 cloves chopped garlic, 1 teaspoon chopped fresh parsley, 4 Tablespoons tahina*, a pinch of salt, juice of 1 lemon. Mix well and then drizzle olive oil over the mixture. Scoop a bite with a piece of pita bread. A great Arab snack and always present at mezas*.

*Tahina is a paste made from ground sesame seeds and is common now in food stores. *Meza is a selection of small dishes or finger food that is part of an Arab meal.

Conclusion

Well. You have had a guided tour of my garden. A journey through time, history, problems, ideas, choices, some botany slipped in there and we ended up with vegetables.

Researching opened doors for me on the everyday varieties of vegetables that were bred in the US and the companies that developed from innovative farmers. It is something to be proud of and to celebrate.

My intent for the reader is to walk away with the knowledge that vegetables are not dull or boring. They have personalities, beauty with a long history.

In developing a garden, size is not important, it will bring you in contact with your terrain. There is a partnership that is achieved, a level of conscientiousness that you are slipping into a system of productive life. You are not the top dog subjugating everything around you but working within it. The soil, plants and animals will all respond to your attention.

But a garden is more than just a plot to produce food. It is a place for experimenting new varieties and new methods. It provides stress free and welcomed solitude, a quiet nook to sit, watching insects and birds interact among the plants. It is a venue giving a small sense of accomplishment and self-sufficiency. An area that is conducive to gathering thoughts, plans, hopes and prayers. A quiet interlude where that voice inside your head is clear and loud with a message. A message of '*I Can Do This.*'

So in effect we have come full circle back to the monastic garden.

A place that provides sustenance, food for the body and soul. My hope and intent is to spark interest and a drive to try your hand at vegetable gardening. You might be surprised by the doors that open up to you.

Are you wondering what my garden actually looks like? Here is a small portion of it.

It is a combination of planting in the ground, in pots and some vertical growing. Herbs and flowers are planted among different vegetables. Some are planted close together but then there are open areas for accessibility but also air circulation. There are some short rows of plantings but I keep them at a minimum.

As an example, located in the foreground are sunflowers, dill, orach, beans, chard and nasturtium. This is intercropping/companion planting. I invite in pollinators and good insects and I hope to discourage and confuse the bad insects. Most of the time it works. Life is not absolute, especially in the gardening world. Happy Gardening!

Bibliography

Allen, Stewart Lee. In the Devil's Garden. Ballantine Publishing Group, 2002.

Andrews, Jean. Peppers. The Domesticated Capsicums. University of Texas Press, 1984. Brady, Nyle C. and Ray R. Well. The Nature and Properties of Soils. Eleventh Edition. Prentice-Hall Inc, 1996.

Braudel, Fernand. The Structures of Everyday Life. Civilization & Capitalism 15th-18th Century. Volume 1. Harper & Row Publishers, 1979.

Brears Peter, Maggie Black, Gill Corbishley, Jane Renfrew and Jennifer Stead. A Taste of History. 10,000 Years of Food in Britain. British Museum Press, 1993.

Chalker-Scott, Linda. The Informed Gardener. University of Washington Press, 2008.

Chalker-Scott, Linda. How Plants Work. The Science Behind the Amazing Things Plants Do. Timber Press, 2015.

Chamovitz, Daniel. What a Plant Knows. A Field Guide to the Senses. Scientific American / Farrar, Straus and Giroux, 2012.

Creasy, Rosalind. The Edible Flower Garden. Periplus Editions, 1999. Crosby Jr, Alford W. The Columbian Exchange. Praeger Publishers, 2003.

Cunningham, Sally Jean. Great Garden Companions. A Companion Planting System for a Beautiful, Chemical-Free, Vegetable Garden. Rodale Press, 1998.

Fenton, Carroll Lane and Herminie B. Kitchen. Plants that Feed Us. The Story of Grains and Vegetables. E. M. Hale and Company, 1961.

Ficklen, Ellen. Watermelon. The Library of Congress, 1984.

Foster, Nelson & Linda S. Cordell. Chilies to Chocolate. Food the Americas Gave the World. The University of Arizona Press, 1992.

Fowler, Cary. Seeds On Ice. Svalbard and the Global Seed Vault. Prospecta Press, 2016.

Gentilcore, David. Pomodoro! A History of the Tomato in Italy. Columbia University Press, 2010.

Goldman, Amy. Melons for the Passionate Grower. Artisan, 2002.
Green, Bert. Green on Green. Workman Publishing, 1984.

Gregory, James John Howard. Carrots, Mangold Wurtzels and Sugar Beets. How to Raise Them, How to Keep Them and How to Feed Them. Reprinted by Forgotten Books, a registered trademark of Fb &c Ltd, 2018. Originally published by Messenger Steam Printing House, 1882.

Hales, Mick. Monastic Gardens. Stewart, Tabori & Chang, 2000.

Hanson, Thor. The Triumph of Seeds. How Grains, Nuts, Kernels, Pulses, & Pips Conquered the Plant Kingdom and Shaped Human History. Basic Books, 2015.

Heiser Jr., Charles B. Nightshades. The Paradoxical Plants. W. H. Freeman and Company, 1969.

Heiser Jr., Charles B. Seed to Civilization. The Story of Food. Second Edition. W. H. Freeman and Company, 1981.

Heiser Jr., Charles B. Of Plants and People. University of Oklahoma

Press, 1985.

Kiple, Kenneth F. & Kriemhild Conee Ornelas. The Cambridge World History of Food. Volumes One & Two. Cambridge University Press, 2000.

Kiple, Kenneth F. A Movable Feast. Ten Millennia of Food Globalization. Cambridge University Press, 2013.

Kohnke, Helmut and D. P. Franzmeier. Soil Science Simplified. Fourth Edition. Waveland Press, 1995.

Landsberg, Sylvia. The Medieval Garden. British Museum Press, 1996.

Laudan, Rachel. Cuisine & Empire. Cooking in World History. University of California Press, 2013.

Laws, Bill. Artists' Gardens. Trafalgar Square Publishing, 1999.

Laws, Bill. Spade, Skirret and Parsnip. The Curious History of Vegetables. Sutton Publishing, 2004.

Laws, Bill. Fifty Plants that Changed the Course of History. David & Charles Ltd, 2010.

LeHoullier, Craig. Epic Tomatoes. How to Select & Grow the Best Varieties of All Time. Storey Publishing, 2015.

McLean, Teresa. Medieval English Gardens. Dover Publications Inc, 1980.

Mennell, Stephen. All Manners of Food. Eating and Taste in England and France from the Middle Ages to the Present. Basil Blackwell Inc, 1987.

Montgomery, David R. Growing a Revolution. Bringing Our Soil Back to Life. W. W. Norton & Company, 2017.

Page, John. Grow the Best Tomatoes. Revised and Updated. Storey Publishing, LLC, 1998. Pollan, Michael. Second Nature. A Gardener's Education. Grove Press, 1991.

Pollan, Michael. The Botany of Desire. Random House Trade Paperback Edition, 2001.

Pollan, Michael. Omnivore's Dilemma. A Natural History of Four Meals. Penguin Books, 2006.

Pollan, Michael. In Defense of Food. An Eater's Manifesto. Penguin Books. 2008. Pollan, Michael. Food Rules. An Eater's Manual. Penguin Books, 2009.

Raman, Tina / Ewa-Marie Rundquist / Justine Lagache. Good Soil. Manure, Compost and Nourishment for Your Garden. Frances LIncoln, 2017.

Randolph, Mary. The Virginia Housewife Or Methodical Cook. A Facsimile of An Authentic Early American Cookbook. Dover Publication, 1993. Originally published by E. H. Butler, 1860.

Reichard, Sarah Hayden. The Conscientious Gardener. Cultivating a Garden Ethic. University of California Press, 2011.

Rupp, Rebecca. How Carrots Won the Trojan War. Curious (but true) Stories of Common Vegetables. Storey Publishing, 2011.

Simmons, Amelia. The First American Cookbook. A Facsimile of "American Cookery," 1796. Dover Publishing, 1984.

Slater, Nigel. Tender. A Cook and His Vegetable Patch. Ten Speed

Press, 2009.

Stone, Daniel. The Food Explorer. The True Adventures of the Globe-Trotting Botanist Who Transformed What America Eats. Dutton, 2018.

Swain, Roger B. Groundwork. A Gardener's Ecology. Houghton Mifflin Company, 1994. Tannahill, Reay. Food in History. Three Rivers Press, 1988.

Tinniswood, Adrian. Life in the English Country Cottage. Weidenfeld & Nicolson, 1995.

Toussaint-Samat, Maguelonne. Translated by Anthea Bell. History of Food. Blackwell Publishers Inc, 1998.

Weaver, William Woys. Heirloom Vegetable Gardening. A Master Gardener's Guide to Planting, Seed Saving and Cultural History. Henry Holt and Company Inc, 1997.

Weaver, William Woys. 100 Vegetables and Where They Came From. Algonquin Books of Chapel Hill, 2000.

Weaver, William Woys. Heirloom Vegetable Gardening, A Master Gardener's Guide to Planting, Seed Saving and Cultural History. Quarto Publishing Group, 2018.

Wheaton, Barbara Ketcham. Savoring the Past. The French Kitchen and Table from 1300 to 1789. The University of Pennsylvania Press, 1983.

Whitaker, Thomas Wallace and Glen N. Davis. Cucurbits. Botany, Cultivation and Utilization. Biotech Books, 2012.

Wright, Clifford A. Mediterranean Vegetables. A Cook's

Compendium of All the Vegetables From the World's Healthiest Cuisine. The Harvard Common Press, 2001.

Websites

Cornell University. http://www.gardening.cornell.edu

Kew Gardens. https://www.kew.org/search?textsearch=vegetables

Missouri Botanical Garden.
https://www.missouribotanicalgarden.org

Mother Earth News. https://www.motherearthnews.com/

Oregon State University.
https://extension.oregonstate.edu>gardening

Washington State University.
https://pubs.extension.wsu.edu>gardening

Xerces Society. http://www.xerces.org/milkweed/milkweed-guides

Seed Sources

- Adaptive Seeds
- Baker Creek Heirloom Seeds
- Botanic
- Botanical Interest Seeds
- Deep Harvest Seeds
- Ferry-Morse
- Franchi Seeds

Johnny's

Maurrie's Garden

Renee's Garden

Seed Savers Exchange

Seeds Trust

Southern Exposure Seed Exchange

Territorial Seeds

www.ingramcontent.com/pod-product-compliance
Lightning Source LLC
Chambersburg PA
CBHW041316110526
44591CB00021B/2803